kevin
mayhew

First published in 2004 by

KEVIN MAYHEW LTD
Buxhall, Stowmarket, Suffolk, IP14 3BW
E-mail: info@kevinmayhewltd.com

KINGSGATE PUBLISHING INC
1000 Pannell Street, Suite G, Columbia, MO 65201
E-mail: sales@kingsgatepublishing.com

The material in this book first appeared in *Selected Prayers
for Public Worship* and *Short Prayers for Public Worship*.

9 8 7 6 5 4 3 2 1 0

ISBN 1 84417 250 3
Catalogue No. 1500700

Cover design by Angela Selfe
Edited by Peter Dainty
Typesetting by Louise Selfe

Printed and bound in Great Britain

Contents

Acknowledgement

I am indebted to Peter Dainty for his careful selection of these prayers, undertaken with typical thoroughness and wisdom. Over many years, Peter's reports on my various manuscripts submitted to Kevin Mayhew Ltd have proven invaluable, saving me from many an error, offering innumerable constructive suggestions, and helping to develop my style as a writer. I could not have wished for wiser or more beneficial counsel.

_____ Foreword _____

Following the publication of *Short Prayers for Public Worship* and *Selected Prayers for Public Worship* it was suggested that the material within them might usefully be adapted for personal devotions. The result is this book. Arranged thematically to assist the reader, each of the prayers has been carefully adapted and revised for individual use. Generally, of course, we will tend to use our own words in prayer, and it is right that we should, for ultimately all prayer is a personal matter between the individual and God. No one can tell us how to pray, still less fully articulate all our thoughts and feelings. Yet, having said that, there are times when prayer doesn't come as easily as we would like, or when, in the press of a busy day, we simply do not have sufficient time prayerfully to gather our thoughts. At such moments, a resource of prayer to turn to can be immensely useful, helping us meaningfully yet simply to consecrate time to God. I remember my college principal, years back when I was training for the ministry, emphasising that point, urging all students to put together a collection of prayer books and other material to nourish and enrich their prayer life. I have never forgotten that advice, its wisdom repeatedly reinforced during my time in the pastoral ministry. This book, then, is offered not as a substitute for, but as a supplement to, personal prayer. It is my hope that, through using it in whatever ways seem appropriate, it will help to nurture and express your ongoing relationship with God.

NICK FAWCETT

Christian seasons

Advent

1

Lord Jesus Christ,
   I remember during this Advent season
   that though your people longed
   for your coming,
   many were not prepared to welcome you,
   failing to recognise you when you came.
Forgive me that I am equally closed sometimes
   to your coming into my life,
   forcing you into a mould I have made for you,
   presuming your thoughts and your ways
   are the same as mine.
Forgive me that my expectations are small and limited,
   shaped by looking at life from a human
   rather than eternal perspective.
Forgive me,
   and help me to be prepared.
Teach me to examine myself –
   my words and deeds,
   thoughts and attitudes –
   and so to live each day open to what you would do
   in me and through me,
   to the glory of your name.
Amen.

2

Loving God,
   I praise you that the light which dawned
   in the life of Zechariah and Elizabeth,
   that transformed the future for Mary and Joseph,
   and that lit up the sky

on the night of the Saviour's birth,
continues to shine today.
I thank you for the joy
your love has brought into our lives,
and the light of your gospel that continues to guide us.
Teach me to walk in that light day by day,
and so may each moment be a new dawn,
a new beginning,
rich in promise and filled by your love,
through Jesus Christ my Lord.
Amen.

3
Loving God,
the great festival of Christmas is drawing nearer
and I am busy preparing for it –
choosing presents,
writing cards,
planning get-togethers,
buying food –
so much that has become an accepted
and expected part of this season.
Yet, in all the bustle, I so easily forget what matters most:
responding to the gift of your Son.
Forgive me for relegating Jesus
to the periphery of my celebrations
rather than placing him at the centre where he belongs;
for doing so much to prepare for Christmas
on the surface
yet so little to make myself ready within.
Open my heart to welcome the living Christ into my life,
and so may I rejoice in his love,
not just at Christmas,
but always.
In his name I ask it.
Amen.

4

Gracious God,
    I praise you for this season of Advent,
    this time for rejoicing and celebration,
    for praise and worship,
    for exulting in your goodness.
I praise you for coming in Christ,
    bringing in a new kingdom
    and anticipating an era of peace and justice
    when the poor will have plenty,
    the hungry be fed, and the lowly be lifted up.
I praise you that you want me to be a part of that,
    not just to share in it
    but also to play a part in bringing it to pass.
Forgive me that I sometimes lose sight of your purpose
    and underestimate your greatness.
Open my eyes to the breadth of your love,
    the wonder of your mercy
    and the extent of your goodness,
    and so may I give you the worship and adoration
    that is due to you, this and every day,
    through Jesus Christ my Lord.
Amen.

5

Lord Jesus Christ,
    teach me to anticipate your return
    by preparing the way for your coming;
    to catch a glimpse of your kingdom
    through living by its values today.
Live in me now,
    so that the day may come when I live with you
    and all your people for all eternity,
    your will complete and your promise fulfilled.
In your name I ask it.
Amen.

6

Lord Jesus Christ,
>   I look forward to that day
>   when your kingdom shall come and you are all in all.
Until then, I will trust in you,
>   secure in your love, confident in your eternal purpose,
>   assured that your will shall be done.
To you be praise and glory,
>   now and for evermore.
Amen.

Christmas

7

Gracious God,
>   help me to learn from the example of Mary.
Teach me this Christmastime
>   to ponder, as she did, all that you have said and done:
>   to listen again to familiar readings and carols,
>   and to hear again the story I know so well,
>   but also to consider what it all might mean;
>   what you are saying not just to others but also to me.
Amid all the celebrations and rejoicing,
>   help me to be still before you
>   so that I may open my heart to your living word,
>   your renewing love
>   and your redeeming power,
>   and so know the presence of Jesus within me,
>   by his grace.
Amen.

8

Gracious God,
>   I thank you for the joy of Christmastime:
>   the joy you gave to Mary, the shepherds and the magi
>   as you entered the world in Christ;

the joy you have brought
to generations across the centuries
as they have come to faith;
the joy you offer us now
in a living and saving knowledge of Jesus Christ.
I praise you that, whatever I face,
you are with me through him,
supporting me by your love,
enriching me by your grace,
equipping me through your Spirit.
Inspire me afresh each day with the good news of Christ
and the reality of his presence in my heart,
and so may I go on my way rejoicing,
now and always.
Amen.

9
Loving God,
I thank you for the great truth
at the heart of this season –
your coming to this world in Christ.
I praise you that you go on coming,
day after day,
not just to others but also to me,
meeting and working within me
through your Holy Spirit.
Forgive me everything that obstructs your coming –
all the trivia and irrelevancies with which I fill my life
at the cost of time for you;
all the cares, doubts and unbelief
that prevent me sometimes
from even glimpsing your presence.
Come afresh now,
and break through all the barriers in my life,
so that I may know you more nearly by my side

and draw yet closer to you
than I have ever been before.
Speak your word,
   grant your guidance,
   confer your power
   and fill me with your love,
   so that I may serve you as faithfully
   as you have served the world in Christ.
In his name I ask it.
Amen.

10
Living God,
   teach me that the joyful message
   proclaimed at Bethlehem all those years ago
   is good news for me today,
   here and now.
Amen.

11
Lord Jesus,
   child in the manger,
   man on the cross,
   risen Saviour,
   Lord of all,
   be born in me today.
Amen.

Epiphany

12
Lord Jesus Christ,
   you have told us to seek and we shall find.
Yet that search is not always easy.
As I look for meaning in my life,
   there is so much that puzzles and perplexes.

The more I discover,
    the more I realise how little I have understood.
Give me the determination of the wise men
    to keep on looking,
    despite all that obscures you,
    until at last I find my perseverance rewarded
    and, glimpsing your glory,
    I kneel before you in joyful worship.
Amen.

13

Sovereign God,
    I am reminded today of the journey of the magi:
    of how they stepped out into the unknown,
    persevering despite adversity,
    searching diligently until their quest was rewarded.
I also come seeking:
    looking to learn from their experience,
    to worship the one before whom they knelt in homage,
    to understand what his birth, life, death
    and resurrection mean for me.
Help me to discover each day a little more of your love,
    and to discern more of your gracious purpose,
    and so, in turn,
    may I offer you each moment a little more of my life,
    in joyful thanks
    and glad thanksgiving
    through Jesus Christ my Lord.
Amen.

Lent

14

Almighty and all-seeing God,
    I thank you for this season of Lent:
    a time to reflect upon my discipleship,
    to consider my calling,

to examine myself
and to assess the health of my faith.
Help me to be honest in this:
to see myself as I really am
with all my weaknesses, ugliness and sinfulness.
Help me to face the things I usually prefer to push aside;
the unpleasant truths I sweep under the carpet,
pretending they are not there.
Help me to come to you now,
acknowledging my faults,
recognising my weaknesses
and receiving your forgiveness,
which alone can make me whole,
through the grace of Christ.
Amen.

15
Lord Jesus Christ,
sometimes you present me with a choice:
between right and wrong,
good and evil,
life and death.
I know the way I ought to take,
but I know also the cost,
so I hold back,
passing the buck instead to others.
Yet eventually I cannot evade your challenge,
for in the very act of avoiding I make my decision.
Lord Jesus Christ,
give me courage to face the choices life brings,
and give me wisdom to choose the right way.
Amen.

16
Living God,
it's easy to fool myself that I am observing Lent –

giving up certain vices,
denying myself particular pleasures,
and making fine-sounding resolutions –
but deep down I know that Lent
should be more than this:
a time rather for prayer and reflection,
for self-examination and renewed commitment.
I come, then, seeking your will,
your word,
your guidance
and your grace.
Nurture my feeble faith
and help me to put you at the centre of this season,
so that through it I may know you better,
love you more fully
and serve you more effectively,
to the glory of your name.
Amen.

17

Gracious God,
despite my resolve to serve you
I am so easily led astray.
Like a foolish sheep,
I blindly follow the example of the crowd.
I congratulate myself on resisting
the latest trend or fashion,
but the pressures to conform
are more subtle than that,
often unseen,
unrecognised.
Help me to listen to *you*
rather than the voices that surround me,
to stay close to *your* side and respond to *your* guidance.
And, should I find myself lost,
seek me out through Christ, the Good Shepherd,

and restore me to your fold,
for his name's sake.
Amen.

18

Lord Jesus Christ,
   you faced temptation in the wilderness –
   enticement to put yourself first,
   to seek worldly glory,
   to compromise your calling –
   and steadfastly you refused.
You faced pressure throughout your ministry –
   hostility,
   ridicule,
   threats,
   rejection –
   yet you carried on regardless,
   true to your message,
   true to your mission.
You faced the greatest test of all in Gethsemane,
   as you wrestled there
   with the prospect of betrayal, denial,
   suffering and death,
   but once again you held firm,
   putting God's will before your own.
What you said and what you did were always one,
   each testifying to the other.
Lord Jesus Christ,
   I fall so short of that goal,
   words coming easily,
   deeds to match rarely coming at all.
Forgive me,
   and help me to show in my life
   the things I proclaim with my lips,
   for your name's sake.
Amen.

19

Gracious God,
    teach me to wrestle with my sin,
    my doubts,
    my fears and my weaknesses,
    and, in battling with those,
    may I find I have taken hold of you,
    through Christ my Lord.
Amen.

Palm Sunday

20

Lord Jesus Christ,
    on Palm Sunday I am reminded
    of how you entered Jerusalem
    to shouts of joy and celebration.
But I remember too how quickly
    that welcome evaporated,
    how soon the mood of the crowd changed.
Lord Jesus Christ,
    I know all too well that I am little different,
    my commitment to you so often short-lived,
    superficial,
    self-centred.
Help me to welcome you into my life with true gladness,
    and to go on serving you come what may,
    now and always.
Amen.

21

Lord Jesus Christ,
    as I remember your triumphant entry into Jerusalem,
    I am reminded of how easy it would have been
    for you to take the easy option,
    to follow the way of the world.

With the shouts of welcome still ringing in your ears,
 the hosannas of the crowd still fresh in your memory,
 it must have been so tempting
 to give them what they wanted,
 to be the sort of Messiah they hoped you would be.
But with you there was no compromise,
 no watering down of your message
 for the sake of popular acclaim.
You stayed true to your calling
 despite the inevitable consequences.
Lord,
 I find it so hard to stay true in turn,
 so difficult not to bend a little here
 and give a little there.
Give me courage to walk the way of discipleship,
 and, by your grace, to stay true to you
 come what may.
In your name I pray.
Amen.

Holy Week

22
Loving God,
 through your Son you walked the way of the cross,
 each step leading you inexorably to suffering,
 humiliation and death.
I know it,
 and yet I continue to marvel,
 for such love defies human logic,
 transcending anything I can give in return.
Open my heart afresh to the wonder of your love,
 and help me to glimpse more fully all it cost you
 and all it offers to me.
So help me to respond,
 with a grateful heart

in joyful service,
to the glory of your name.
Amen.

23

Lord Jesus Christ,
　you gave so much;
　forgive me that I give so little.
You refused to count the cost;
　I resent even the smallest sacrifice being asked of me.
You took the way of others;
　I take the way of self.
Lord Jesus,
　all good, all loving,
　I have no claim on your goodness,
　no reason to expect your mercy,
　yet, despite that, still you died for me.
Have mercy, I pray,
　and, poor though it may be,
　accept the discipleship I offer,
　and use me in the service of your kingdom,
　to the glory of your name.
Amen.

24

Lord Jesus Christ,
　you didn't take the *easy* way as we would have done:
　the path of popular acclaim,
　of least resistance.
You took the *right* way:
　the way of truth, love and service,
　and you followed it faithfully,
　knowingly,
　undeterred by the consequences,
　intent on serving others rather than yourself.

Forgive me that I am so easily led astray,
   thinking so much for myself and so little for you.
Forgive me for my willingness to compromise,
   even when I know the way I ought to take.
Strengthen my resolve,
   increase my faith,
   and help me to stay true to my calling and true to you,
   to the glory of your name.
Amen.

Good Friday

25

Lord Jesus Christ,
   I marvel again today at your astonishing love:
   the way you endured the humiliation of Gethsemane,
   the agony of the cross
   and the darkness of the tomb,
   not because you *had* to
   but because you *chose* to.
I praise you that, despite the jeers and ridicule you faced,
   your concern was always for others
   rather than yourself,
   and thus you freely chose the way of humility,
   service and self-sacrifice:
   the lonely path of the cross.
Above all,
   I praise you for your faithfulness to the last –
   that though you could so easily
   have stepped down from the cross,
   you didn't;
   and though you could have saved yourself,
   you preferred instead to save the world.
Lord Jesus Christ,
   however often I hear it,

    still I am amazed by the magnitude of your love
    and the awesomeness of your sacrifice.
Receive my praise and accept my worship,
    for your name's sake.
Amen.

26

Lord Jesus Christ,
    you suffered so much for our sakes –
    pain of mind as well as body:
    the pain of waiting for the end,
    of mockery and rejection,
    of betrayal, denial and misunderstanding,
    of flogging and physical blows,
    of thorns pressed on to your head
    and nails driven into your hands and feet,
    of hanging in agony on that cross.
Lord Jesus Christ,
    as I celebrate all you have given,
    help me never to forget what it cost.
Amen.

27

Loving God,
    I praise you that in Jesus
    you experienced not just life but also death –
    that you endured the darkness of Gethsemane,
    the agony of the cross
    and the finality of the tomb,
    triumphing over everything that keeps us from you.
I thank you that where the world saw only defeat,
    you brought victory,
    nothing able to stand against your sovereign purpose.
May that knowledge bring hope
    to all for whom life is overshadowed by death;

a new perspective bringing light
into the pain and sorrow of such moments.
Grant the assurance that death is not the end
but a new beginning,
a stepping stone into your glorious kingdom
in which death shall be no more
and where all will rejoice in the wonder of your love,
for evermore.
Amen.

Easter

28

Lord Jesus Christ,
like the two disciples on the Emmaus Road,
so often I journey through life
unaware of your presence.
Though I talk of your resurrection
it does not stir my heart or capture my imagination
in the way it should.
Yet even though I may not realise it,
you are there with me,
matching your stride to mine,
waiting to meet me along the way.
Open my eyes
that I may see and know you better.
Amen.

29

Lord Jesus Christ,
I rejoice today in the good news of your resurrection.
You met with Mary in the garden,
bringing laughter after tears.
You met with women returning from the tomb,
bringing confidence after confusion.

You met with Cleopas on the Emmaus Road,
    bringing hope after despair.
You met with the Apostles
    in a room barred against the world,
    bringing joy after sorrow.
You met with Thomas, in his disbelief,
    bringing faith after doubt.
You met with Paul on his way to Damascus,
    bringing love after hatred.
You met with countless generations across the centuries,
    bringing renewal after rejection.
Meet with me now, in this day, this moment,
    bringing light after darkness.
Fill my heart with the new life of Easter,
    until that day when, with all your people,
    I enter your kingdom
    and rejoice in the wonder of your love for all eternity.
In your name I pray.
Amen.

30
Living God,
    I praise you for the great truth of Easter –
    the message that your love will not be defeated.
When human evil had done its worst,
    despite every effort to frustrate your purpose,
    still your will triumphed!
The stone was rolled away,
    the tomb was empty,
    Christ had risen!
May that truth fire me each day with new hope,
    new confidence,
    and new enthusiasm,
    knowing that whatever obstacles I may face
    and whatever may fight against me,
    there is nothing that will finally

be able to thwart your purpose
or to deny your saving purpose,
in Jesus Christ my Lord.
Amen.

31
Living God,
   I praise you for the wonder of Easter –
   this day that changed the world for ever!
I rejoice in the victory of Christ:
   his triumph over evil,
   hatred,
   despair,
   and even death itself.
Living God,
   I praise you for the victory you have won,
   and for the assurance it brings
   that nothing in life or death
   can ever separate me from your love;
   nothing in heaven or earth
   defeat your loving purpose for all the world.
To you be praise and glory,
   this day and always.
Amen.

32
Living God,
   I praise you once more for the good news of Easter,
   the triumphant message of resurrection –
   new hope,
   new joy,
   new life!
I praise you for the truth at its heart:
   that your love could not be kept down,
   your purpose could not be defeated
   and your mercy could not be destroyed.

Teach me that what was true then is true now –
    that nothing can stand in the way
    of your sovereign power and redeeming grace.
Assure me, then,
    even when faith seems to fly in the face of reason,
    to trust in you,
    confident that your will shall be done
    and your kingdom come,
    through Jesus Christ my Lord.
Amen.

33

Lord Jesus Christ,
    I thank you for the great message of Easter –
    that in what the world counted defeat
    you won the greatest of victories.
I praise you for your triumph over evil and death,
    and for everything this has meant over the years
    to so many people.
Most of all,
    I thank you for my own experiences
    of your resurrection power –
    the times you have brought me victory
    over all that stops me living life to the full.
Teach me to live each day
    in the light of what you have done,
    confident that no situation,
    however dreadful it may seem,
    is finally beyond your power to redeem,
    and so may I put my trust in you always,
    for this life, and the life to come.
Amen.

34

Living God,
    I look at the world and at my life

and I am dismayed sometimes
at how little seems to change.
I go on making the same mistakes I've always made,
and all around me there seems to be
as much sorrow, suffering,
hatred and evil as there has ever been.
Help me to hold on to the conviction
that things can change;
to remember how,
in the resurrection of Christ,
you overcame the power of sin and death.
Help me to remember that
though everything may seem to conspire against you,
you have won the victory through him –
a victory that nothing can ever undo –
and so may I trust in your ability
to transform and renew all things,
by his grace.
Amen.

Ascension

35

Lord Jesus Christ,
teach me what it means to acknowledge you as Lord.
Help me to offer you the worship you deserve:
to bring you my praise and homage,
and to acknowledge you as King of kings
and Lord of lords.
But help me also to offer you the service you deserve:
to respond to everything you have done for me
through working wholeheartedly for your kingdom,
committing myself body, mind and soul
to the fulfilment of your purpose
and the making known of your love.

Take me,
   and use me as you will,
   for your glory.
Amen.

36

Lord Jesus Christ,
   I claim to follow you,
   and I declare you to be the Lord and King of my life,
   but all too often my actions deny my words.
I have broken your commandments,
   betrayed your love
   and ignored your guidance –
   my faith fickle and my allegiance poor.
Forgive me all the ways I fail you,
   through thought, word and deed.
Forgive me my limited understanding
   of your greatness
   and the narrowness of my vision.
Forgive my inability to grasp the values
   of your kingdom,
   still less to base my life upon them.
Lord Jesus,
   I come before your throne,
   throwing myself upon your grace,
   and asking you to receive my homage and service,
   poor though these may be.
Rule in my heart
   and use me for the growth of your kingdom,
   to the glory of your name.
Amen.

37

Baby of Bethlehem, born in a stable,
   I worship you.
Child of Nazareth, full of grace and truth,
   I acknowledge you.

Man of Galilee, teacher, preacher, healer, redeemer,
    I praise you.
Son of David, coming in humility to claim your kingdom,
    I greet you.
Suffering servant, bruised, beaten, broken,
    I salute you.
Lord of the empty tomb, risen and triumphant,
    I honour you.
King of kings, exalted by the side of the Father,
    I adore you.
Jesus Christ, my Lord and Saviour,
    receive the homage I offer,
    to the glory of your name.
Amen.

38

Lord Jesus Christ,
    you are greater than I can ever imagine,
    before all,
    beyond all,
    in all
    and over all.
Forgive me for losing sight of your greatness;
    for underestimating the breadth of your love
    and the extent of your purpose;
    for tying you down to the things of earth
    rather than opening my heart
    to the kingdom of heaven.
Broaden my vision,
    enlarge my understanding,
    deepen my faith,
    kindle my imagination,
    that I may glimpse your glory,
    and work more faithfully for your kingdom.
In your name I ask it.
Amen.

39

Lord Jesus Christ,
   you were brought low,
   yet you have been lifted high.
You were the servant of all,
   yet you are above all and beyond all.
You were despised and rejected,
   yet your name is exalted above all names.
You were fully human,
   yet you are divine.
You were taken into heaven,
   yet you are here by my side.
You are higher than my highest thoughts,
   yet I can know you as a friend.
So, with all your people in every age,
   I bow before you
   and confess you as my risen Saviour,
   the King of kings and Lord of lords,
   to the glory of God the Father.
Amen.

Pentecost

40

Living God,
   I remember today how you transformed
   the lives of the Apostles:
   how, through the breath of your Spirit,
   you turned their fear into confidence,
   their weakness into strength,
   their doubt into faith,
   and their sorrow into joy.
Come to me now, through that same Spirit.
Take my weak and hesitant faith
   and fill me with unshakeable trust in your purpose.

Take my stumbling discipleship,
    and grant me energy and enthusiasm
    to proclaim the gospel through word and deed.
Take my fear and anxieties,
    and give me courage
    and your peace that passes understanding.
Take my gifts and talents,
    and use them in the service of your kingdom.
Living God,
    help me to remember today
    not simply all you did *once*,
    but to rejoice in all you are doing *now*
    and all you shall continue to do
    through your Holy Spirit.
In the name of Christ I ask it.
Amen.

41
Gracious God,
    I thank you that I can know you for myself
    through the living presence of your Holy Spirit.
I praise you that, by your Spirit,
    you meet my innermost needs,
    filling my soul to overflowing with joy,
    peace,
    hope
    and power.
I celebrate the way you are always moving in my life,
    deepening my faith,
    enriching my experience,
    strengthening my commitment
    and enlarging my vision.
Help me to open my life more fully
    to the presence of your Spirit,
    so that I may know you better

and be equipped to serve you more fully,
to the glory of your name.
Amen.

42
Lord Jesus Christ,
I know what fruits you would like to see in my life:
love,
joy,
peace,
patience,
kindness,
generosity,
faithfulness,
gentleness
and self-control.
I know I ought to show these,
but I know also how rarely I do,
how all too often the fruits I yield
are so very different.
Instead of living by the Spirit I live by the flesh,
and the results are plain for all to see.
Forgive me,
and by your grace grant me another chance
to start again.
Put your Spirit within me
and nurture my faith,
so that the time will come
when my life will bear a rich harvest
to the glory of your name.
Amen.

43
Holy Spirit,
unpredictable as the wind,
unquenchable as fire,

yet gentle as a dove:
come now and breathe new energy into my life
and new life into my soul,
by your gracious power.
Amen.

Trinity

44
Mighty God,
beyond all space and time,
greater than my mind can fully grasp,
ruler over all that is and has been and shall be,
I worship you.
I worship you as the God made known in Christ –
a God all good and wholly other,
and yet a God who loves us
as a father loves his children.
I worship you as the God I experience within me –
the God who fires my imagination
and sets my heart aflame through the Spirit of Christ.
Mighty God,
help me to catch a sense of your greatness,
opening my heart and mind to your presence
made known through Father, Son and Holy Spirit.
Amen.

45
Love of the Father, course through my veins.
Goodness of Christ, pulse through my body.
Power of the Spirit, flow through my soul.
Wonder of God, resonate through my mind.
Glory to you, O God, Father, Son and Holy Spirit,
now and for all eternity.
Amen.

46

Loving God,
    equip me through the inner presence
    of your Holy Spirit,
    enrich me through the redeeming grace of Christ,
    and encourage me through the daily experience
    of your fatherly love.
Strengthen my service,
    deepen my faith and enliven my commitment
    so that I may live to your praise and glory.
Amen.

All Saints' Day

47

Living God,
    I thank you for all those who have run the race
    and kept the faith before me;
    all whose example, across the centuries,
    has given encouragement and inspiration
    to your people in their personal journey of faith.
I thank you for those whose life and faith
    have spoken to me –
    uplifting, instructing, challenging and guiding,
    leading me forward
    into new experiences of your love.
Forgive me that I sometimes forget such examples,
    losing sight of all you have done and continue to do.
Help me to learn from the great company of saints
    to which I owe so much.
Speak,
    so that my love may grow,
    my faith be deepened
    and my resolve to serve you be strengthened,
    through Jesus Christ my Lord.
Amen.

48

Lord God,
   you know that life isn't always easy.
There are times when I feel exhausted,
   overwhelmed,
   defeated.
Remind me then of those who have gone before me,
   keeping the faith
   and running the race with perseverance.
Remind me of the fellowship I share
   with all your people,
   and the strength I can gain from others.
Remind me of my responsibility
   to those who will come after me,
   the example I need to set to encourage
   and inspire them.
Above all, remind me of Jesus,
   his willingness to endure the cross for my sake,
   his faithfulness to the end.
So give me strength to battle on,
   in the knowledge that you are waiting to receive me
   and to grant me the joy of your kingdom,
   the prize of everlasting life,
   through Jesus Christ,
   my Lord and Saviour.
Amen.

49

Sovereign God,
   I thank you for all those over the centuries
   who have had the courage to take difficult decisions.
I think of the call of Abram to venture
   into the unknown,
   of Moses to confront the tyranny of Pharaoh,
   of David to take on the might of Goliath,
   of the prophets to declare your word despite hostility,

of the disciples to leave all and follow Jesus,
of Saul to turn from persecutor
to ambassador of the Church.
I thank you for the determination
and the courage these showed;
their willingness to trust in you,
coupled with their readiness to step out in faith,
despite no guarantees as to what
the future might hold.
Speak to me through their example
and through your word,
so that when decisions must be made
I will be ready to make them,
and equipped to choose the right path
through Jesus Christ my Lord.
Amen.

50
Living God,
encourage me through all who have gone before me,
so that I, in turn,
may encourage those who travel after me,
along the way of Christ.
Amen.

Commitment

51

Gracious God,
   I have committed myself to your service,
   but I am all too aware of how weak
   that commitment is
   and how often I fail to honour it.
When my allegiance has been tested,
   my loyalty put on the line,
   I have repeatedly been found wanting,
   more concerned with my own interests
   than with serving Christ.
When discipleship has involved cost,
   and service meant putting myself out
   on behalf of others,
   my good intentions have swiftly evaporated,
   exposed as little more than fine-sounding ideas.
Gracious God,
   I want to serve you better,
   but I know that I will fail again,
   just as I have failed before,
   my faith flawed and my love imperfect.
Have mercy on me,
   and through Christ's faithfulness to the last
   inspire me to stay true to you
   whatever life may bring.
For his name's sake I pray.
Amen.

52

Lord Jesus Christ,
   I want to be true to my convictions,
   to stand up for what is right,
   but it's hard when the pressure is on.

It's hard not to bend when all around me disagree,
    not to compromise for the sake of peace,
    not to tone things down
    when I find myself in the firing line.
Yet there are times when I need to stick my neck out
    for what I believe in,
    even when doing so
    may make me unpopular with others.
Give me wisdom to know when those times are,
    and courage then to hold fast through them all.
Amen.

53

Lord Jesus Christ,
    thank you for staying true to your calling
    to the very end,
    refusing to compromise your mission.
Thank you for all those
    who have followed in your footsteps,
    giving their all for the sake of the gospel.
Teach me to walk faithfully in your way
    rather than follow the course of least resistance,
    to stand up for what I believe
    rather than go along with the crowd.
Help me to understand all you have done for me,
    and so may my life be spent in your service,
    to the glory of your name.
Amen.

54

Lord Jesus Christ,
    I bear your name and I profess to follow your way,
    yet there is little if anything different about me
    from anyone else.
I have failed you in so many ways;
    my faith weak,
    my love poor and my commitment unpredictable.

I have been half-hearted in your service,
   concerned more about my own interests
   than your glory.
All too often my words say one thing
   but my deeds another,
   the message I proclaim belied by the way I live,
   so that instead of leading people towards you
   I lead them away.
Forgive me and help me to follow you
   not just in name only but also in truth,
   proud to be identified with your cause
   and committing my life to the work of your kingdom.
I ask it for your name's sake.
Amen.

55
Lord Jesus Christ,
   I talk about belonging to you
   and offering you my service,
   but so often reality falls short of the ideal.
Instead of making you an integral part of my life,
   I treat you as an optional extra,
   there to turn to as and when it suits me.
Instead of working for your kingdom,
   I strive solely to serve my own interests.
Instead of involving myself in the life of your people,
   I stay on the fringes,
   reluctant to commit myself wholly to your cause.
My deeds deny my words;
   my life betrays my lack of faith.
Forgive me, and save me
   from confusing nominal Christianity
   with living discipleship.
Teach me what it means to belong to you
   and to be part of your Church,

and so may I serve you as you deserve,
to the glory of your name.
Amen.

56

Lord Jesus Christ,
I want to commit myself to your service
and I do my best to follow you,
but I am led astray so easily,
my faith so weak and temptation so strong.
I think I have turned my back on my old ways,
only to find them resurfacing in another guise.
I try to let go of self,
only to discover it still holds me firmly in its grip.
For all my good intentions,
I find myself caught between two worlds,
unable to escape the hold of one
yet incapable of fully embracing the other.
Forgive me the many times I fail you,
and give me strength,
when my allegiance is tested,
to put you first.
Help me not simply to call you Lord,
but also to make you the Lord of my life,
to the glory of your name.
Amen.

57

Loving God,
you ask me, whatever I do,
to do it for your sake –
to offer my whole life,
my every thought,
word and action,
to your service and for your glory.

Help me to understand what that really means –
    to see every part of each day
    as an opportunity to work for you.
Teach me to do everything in such a way
    that your hand may be evident upon me,
    your Spirit unmistakably at work
    and your love clear to all,
    to the glory of your name.
Amen.

58

Sovereign Lord,
    there are things I can do by *myself*
    and things only *you* can do;
    there are times when I have the resources within me
    to cope with a situation
    and times when I depend utterly on you for help.
Teach me to know the difference
    and help me to remember
    that though my reserves may run dry,
    yours never will.
Give me, then, an appreciation of my abilities,
    but, above all, an appreciation of yours,
    through Jesus Christ my Lord.
Amen.

59

Living God,
    I do not risk much today in committing myself to you,
    yet I still do not find it easy,
    for there are many who pour scorn on the gospel,
    who ridicule Christianity,
    and who mock those who profess faith in you.
Still more are dismissive of you;
    not hostile
    but simply regarding Christian teaching

and everything to do with the Church
as an outdated irrelevance.
In some ways I find such apathy and indifference
harder to cope with than outright rejection,
for no one likes being thought foolish,
and as a result I am tempted
to compromise my convictions,
to tone down my message
or even to conceal my commitment.
Help me to remember that your wisdom
is often counted by the world as foolishness,
and to remember in turn
that the wisdom of this world
is all too often folly.
Give me the courage and dedication I need
to stay true to you
no matter what people may say or think –
the faith, if necessary, to be a fool for Christ.
Amen.

60
Sovereign God,
you tell us that from those who have been given much,
much will be expected in turn.
Forgive me for forgetting sometimes
the second part of that challenge,
rejoicing in your goodness,
celebrating your gift of life
and the new life you offer in Christ,
but forgetting that all this brings responsibility
as well as privilege,
and that one day I will be called to account
for the way I have lived and acted.
Teach me, then, to live wisely,
responding to your guidance
and doing your will,

even though, in this life,
everything may seem to count against it.
Help me to be faithful to you,
as you are faithful to me,
through Jesus Christ my Lord.
Amen.

61

Gracious God,
I do not know you or serve you as I should,
my faith sometimes short both on theory and practice.
I am careless in making time for you,
rarely stopping to read your word or seek your will.
I am casual in discipleship,
more concerned with serving myself
than you or others.
Help me to know you better
and to love you more deeply,
and may that in turn help me
to prove my love for you in action,
showing the sincerity of my faith
by practising what I preach,
to the glory of your name.
Amen.

62

Living God,
too easily I turn faith
into a matter of personal devotion and fulfilment,
forgetting that it must show itself in the way I live.
I make time for prayer and worship,
I read and study your word,
but then I fail to go out into the world
and make real there the truth of what I believe.
Forgive me,
and help me to minister in your name,

bringing peace, hope, help and healing,
sharing your love and working
to bring your kingdom closer here on earth.
In the name of Christ I ask it.
Amen.

63

Gracious God,
when the spark of faith starts to flicker
and the fire of commitment grows cold,
rekindle in me the joy with which I first started out,
so that I may awake each day with hope in my heart
and live each moment rejoicing in your love,
to the glory of your name.
Amen.

64

Almighty God,
I commit to you not simply a part but all of life,
asking that you will take who and what I am,
and everything I do,
and dedicate it to your service,
for your name's sake.
Amen.

65

Gracious God,
take my faith, flawed though it is,
my love, poor though it may be,
and my commitment, with all its imperfections,
and use me in your service
to make known your gracious purpose,
through Jesus Christ my Lord.
Amen.

Confession

66

Lord Jesus Christ,
    I do not mean to be self-righteous but I *can* be,
    more often than I realise.
I speak of humility,
    of being wholly dependent on your grace,
    yet I presume to pass judgement on others.
I claim to recognise my faults,
    but if anyone points them out to me
    I am quick to take offence.
I see the speck in my neighbour's eye
    but repeatedly overlook the log in my own.
Forgive any tendency to assume that I am right
    and others are wrong.
Help me, instead,
    to understand that I depend finally on your grace,
    and so, recognising the strengths
    and weaknesses of all,
    may I live in true humility,
    to the glory of your name.
Amen.

67

Lord,
    I don't like being wrong.
It hurts my pride
    and goes against the grain
    to admit I've made a mistake.
I prefer to blame somebody else,
    to look for an excuse that justifies my actions,
    but though I may fool myself,
    I can never fool you.

Forgive me, Lord, for those times
   I have shifted the blame on to others.
Forgive me for hiding behind falsehoods
   and half-truths,
   letting excuses become so much part of me
   that I no longer realise I am making them.
Teach me to act wisely and with integrity;
   and when I go wrong,
   give me courage to admit it
   and humility to accept my dependence
   on your unfailing grace.
Amen.

68

Living God,
   there is so much in my life that is not as it should be,
   yet all too often I stubbornly refuse to admit it.
I pretend that nothing much is wrong;
   that any minor aberrations are superficial,
   hardly worth bothering about.
Even when I am more honest with myself,
   I still believe that I can put matters right
   through my own efforts;
   that all it needs is a greater resolve on my part.
Yet, despite all my attempts to start afresh,
   the old mistakes and weaknesses
   soon show through,
   as unsightly as ever.
Teach me that I need your help
   if I seriously hope ever to change.
Take me and mould me in your hands,
   re-creating me from within,
   so that, by the grace of Christ,
   I may be the person you would have me be.
Amen.

69

Living God,
    though I have let you down in so many ways,
    teach me that you do not judge as I do,
    but that you are truly willing to forgive and forget.
Teach me to put the past behind me
    and to accept the new life you so freely offer,
    and so may I live each day as your gift,
    nurtured by the love of Christ
    and renewed through your Holy Spirit,
    to your praise and glory.
Amen.

70

Lord Jesus Christ,
    you have called me to faith
    and gratefully I have responded,
    committing myself to walking your way,
    yet I am conscious of my repeated failure,
    my inability to keep faith.
I mean to follow,
    but I am weak and foolish,
    so easily deflected from my path,
    and eventually I despair
    of ever staying on my chosen course.
Assure me at such times
    that your patience is never exhausted,
    your love never withdrawn
    and your grace never denied.
Teach me that you long to lead me forward again,
    waiting only for me to acknowledge
    where I have gone wrong
    and to reach out in faith for your forgiveness.
So I come,
    in true repentance,
    asking you to turn me round

and lead me forward,
in your strength
and for your name's sake.
Amen.

71

Loving God,
there are some things in my past I would rather forget
but that return to haunt me:
foolish actions,
hasty words,
evil thoughts,
wasted opportunities –
things I should have done but haven't
or that I shouldn't have done but have.
I find it hard to forgive myself,
harder still to think that others can do so,
and hardest of all to believe
that *you* can ever pardon.
Yet, though I may condemn,
and others may do the same,
you repeatedly show me
how you are able to change lives,
not just forgiving past mistakes
but also making people new,
renewing them from within
through your Holy Spirit.
Help me, then,
to bring all the feelings of guilt and shame
that hold me down,
and to open my life to your renewing touch in Christ,
for in his name I ask it.
Amen.

72

Living God,
you know me inside out down to the last detail.

You see me not as I would like to be,
    nor as I pretend to be,
    but as I am:
    the good and the bad,
    the faithful and the unfaithful,
    the lovely and the unlovely.
I can never deceive you as to the truth,
    never hide the reality of who I am
    behind a public face,
    yet, despite all my faults,
    still you love me.
Living God,
    remembering that truth,
    help me to be honest with you,
    confessing my faults,
    acknowledging my weaknesses
    and seeking your grace,
    through Jesus Christ my Lord.
Amen.

73

Lord Jesus Christ,
    I like to think I have founded my life firmly upon you,
    but the reality may not be as I imagine.
Though I declare my faith and profess your name,
    though I talk of commitment and speak of service,
    there is a danger of this being all show
    and no substance,
    a matter of words rather than deeds.
I fail to listen to what you would tell me,
    I am slow to reflect on what discipleship really means,
    and I offer you only a part of my life,
    keeping the rest back
    for fear of what you might ask of me.
Like the foolish builder,
    I hear your words but do not act upon them,
    my good intentions never translated into action.

Forgive me,
 despite your guidance,
 for building my life on sand rather than rock.
Open my ears,
 my mind and my heart,
 so that I may not only hear
 what you would say to me
 but also respond with body, mind and soul,
 to the glory of your name.
Amen.

74

Merciful God,
 it's not easy being honest with myself,
 for I prefer to keep some things hidden
 rather than face the disturbing truth.
Occasionally I may glimpse my darker side,
 but I push it away,
 attempting to deny its existence even to myself,
 yet the knowledge of my weakness is always there,
 lurking in the shadows.
Help me, then, to open my heart before you
 and to acknowledge my faults,
 in the knowledge that you gave your Son
 to save those who are yet sinners.
Cleanse,
 redeem,
 renew,
 restore,
 and, by your grace,
 help me to come to terms with the person I am,
 so that one day I might become
 the person you would have me be,
 through Jesus Christ my Lord.
Amen.

75

Lord Jesus Christ,
    I talk of following you
    but much of the time I expect *you* to follow *me*.
I want you to conform to my own wishes.
I ask you to meet my list of requirements.
I decide the way I want you to work,
    attempting to mould your purpose
    according to my own narrow horizons.
Lord Jesus Christ,
    break through the chains I put around you,
    and help me to face the searching nature of your truth
    and the challenge it daily brings.
Amen.

76

Lord Jesus Christ,
    I have failed you,
    I have failed myself,
    I have failed others.
Forgive me and help me to live in a way
    that is true to all.
Amen.

Creation

77

Lord of all,
   I forget sometimes that your love
   involves responsibility
   as well as privilege;
   a duty not just to you
   but to the whole of your creation,
   to nurture and protect rather than exploit it.
Forgive me my part in a society
   that has too often lived for today
   with no thought of tomorrow.
Forgive me my unquestioning acceptance
   of an economic system
   that plunders this world's resources
   with little regard as to the consequences.
Help me to live less wastefully
   and with more thought for those
   who will come after me.
Challenge the hearts and minds of people everywhere,
   that both they and I may understand more fully
   the wonder and the fragility of this planet
   you have given us,
   and so honour our calling
   to be faithful stewards of this most precious gift,
   in Christ's name.
Amen.

78

Loving God,
   I thank you for the wonder of the universe
   and the infinite beauty of this world.
I praise you for the loveliness that surrounds me,
   the inexhaustible splendour of creation.

Forgive me for becoming over-familiar with it all,
    exploiting and squandering your many gifts.
Help me to rejoice in all you have given
    and to act as a faithful steward of creation,
    to the glory of your name.
Amen.

79
Creator God,
    I thank you for this world:
    so full of beauty,
    so touched with wonder.
I praise you for its ability to move,
    astound and refresh me,
    and above all for the way it speaks
    of your love and purpose.
Forgive me that I sometimes lose sight
    of those deeper realities,
    failing to look beneath the surface.
Open my eyes afresh,
    and help me to see your hand in creation
    and your love in the daily routine of life,
    through Jesus Christ my Lord.
Amen.

80
Loving God,
    forgive me for taking your many gifts for granted –
    forgetting, squandering and even abusing them.
Help me to rejoice in all you have given
    and to steward it faithfully,
    to your glory.
Amen.

81

In the grandeur of creation but also its simplicity,
    in its power but also its gentleness,
    in all I know but all that yet remains a mystery,
    teach me, O Lord, to glimpse something of you,
    the sovereign hand behind it all.
Amen.

_____ Daily life _____

82

Living God,
  I thank you that before ever I thought of seeking you,
  you sought me;
  that you had time for me
  even when I lived only for myself.
Teach me that you are constantly at work in my life,
  even though I may not always see it,
  speaking through people I meet
  and moving in each and every situation
  to challenge,
  guide,
  confront
  or inspire.
Open my eyes to see you
  and my heart to respond,
  so that I may live and work for your glory,
  through Jesus Christ my Lord.
Amen.

83

Living God,
  I thank you for opportunities to share
  in the worship of your people
  and to focus my thoughts on your presence,
  but save me from mistakenly imagining
  you are more present in worship than anywhere else.
Teach me that you are by my side
  wherever I may be
  and whatever I may be doing,
  involved in every aspect of my life
  and in every part of the world.

May that knowledge illumine the affairs of each day
    and enrich each moment
    as I realise that you are constantly
    waiting to meet with me,
    speak to me,
    lead me
    and bless me.
Teach me to consecrate
    not just a few moments each week
    but all of my life,
    to your service
    and to your glory.
In Christ's name.
Amen.

84

Loving God,
    I thank you for the gift of sight;
    for everything of beauty,
    inspiration and interest that I see each day.
Forgive me, though,
    that too often I see only with my eyes,
    failing to look beneath the surface
    to deeper truths underneath.
Open then my soul,
    so that I may see where you would lead me
    and look at the world in a new light,
    through Jesus Christ my Lord.
Amen.

85

Almighty God,
    teach me to remember all you have done
    and to give you the praise you deserve.
Teach me each day to recall your creative acts,
    your mighty deeds throughout history,

and your faithful dealings
with your people across the years.
Above all, teach me to remember
your graciousness in Jesus Christ –
your coming, living, dying and rising among us,
so that we might have life in all its fullness.
For the memory of such things,
and the constant reminder of them I receive each day,
I give you my thanks and praise,
through Jesus Christ my Lord.
Amen.

86
Sovereign God,
go with me and thrill me afresh each day
by the extent of your love,
the awesomeness of your power,
the generosity of your mercy
and the graciousness of your purpose.
Amen.

Morning

87
Loving God,
thank you for this day
and all the opportunities it will bring:
moments to work and rest,
to give and receive,
to wonder and worship.
Thank you for having been with me
throughout my life –
always there to guide my footsteps
and lead me forward.
Thank you for the assurance
of your continuing guidance –

the knowledge that whatever the future may hold,
whatever challenges I may face or trials I may endure,
you will be there to see me through,
giving me the resources I need to continue,
and a joy that cannot be shaken.
God of past, present and future,
the same yesterday, today and tomorrow,
I praise you for each and every moment,
and consecrate now this day to your service.
In the name of Christ.
Amen.

88

Loving God,
I thank you for the gift of this and every day.
I praise you for all the possibilities each brings,
the innumerable opportunities for love, joy,
fascination and fulfilment that every one opens up.
Teach me to count my blessings
and to welcome this day as your gift,
consecrating it to your service in grateful praise,
through Jesus Christ my Lord.
Amen.

89

Living God,
open my heart to the possibilities of this new day –
to everything it has to offer and, above all,
to all the ways you will be at work within it.
Help me to know and recognise
your living presence at every moment,
and thus live always to your glory,
through Jesus Christ my Lord.
Amen.

90

Sovereign God,
    teach me to live this day to the full
    by living it not just for myself but also,
    and above all, for you.
Amen.

91

Living God,
    show me this day what you would have me do,
    where you would have me go,
    what you would have me say
    and how you would have me serve.
In the name of Christ I ask it.
Amen.

92

Gracious God,
    help me to greet each day as your gift,
    to spend each day in your service,
    to rejoice each day in your love
    and to live each day for your glory,
    through Jesus Christ my Lord.
Amen.

93

Lord Jesus Christ,
    teach me that whatever today may hold
    and whatever tomorrow might bring,
    the future is secure, for you are with me,
    the same yesterday, today and for ever.
Help me, then, to live each moment with you,
    in quiet confidence and joyful celebration,
    knowing that I am yours and you are mine,
    for all eternity.
Amen.

Evening

94

Living God,
   speak to me through everything
   life has brought me today,
   good and bad, pleasure or pain,
   and so help me to be better equipped to serve
   and love you in the days ahead,
   to the glory of your name.
Amen.

95

Gracious God,
   grant rest for my body through this night
   and rest for my soul always.
Amen.

96

Lord Jesus Christ,
   enfold me in your peace,
   encircle me with your love,
   and so may I pass this night
   and live each day in quietness of mind
   and tranquillity of spirit,
   through Jesus Christ my Lord.
Amen.

Discipleship

Journeying

97

Gracious God,
 I thank you for the great adventure of life
 in all its endless diversity and richness.
I thank you that there is always more to learn,
 more to explore
 and more to experience.
Keep my mind open to that special truth
 for, as the years pass,
 I sometimes lose my sense
 of childlike wonder and fascination,
 becoming worldly-wise or blasé about life,
 taking for granted those things
 that once stirred my imagination,
 and so sinking into an ever-deeper
 rut of cynicism and over-familiarity.
Help me to recapture something
 of the innocence and spontaneity
 of my childhood years:
 the ability to look at the world with inquiring eyes,
 to trust in the future
 and to celebrate the present.
Gracious God,
 give me faith in life and faith in you,
 through Jesus Christ my Lord.
Amen.

98

Living God,
 I have committed myself to the path of discipleship
 and I want to walk it faithfully,
 but I know how easy it is to slip back.

Help me to be alert to dangers,
    able to recognise those things that might trip me up.
Help me to keep my eyes on you,
    knowing that you will lead me safely
    through the pitfalls and obstacles in my path.
And, should I stumble or find myself slipping,
    hold on to me,
    keep me steady
    and direct my footsteps
    so that I will find the path once more
    and continue safely on my way
    until my journey's end.
In Christ's name I ask it.
Amen.

99
Lord Jesus Christ,
    you call me,
    as you called your first disciples,
    to follow you:
    not simply to believe,
    nor merely to declare my faith
    and confess you as Lord,
    but to keep on following wherever you lead.
Help me to follow you faithfully,
    following your example,
    pursuing the way of love
    and accepting the road of sacrifice.
Help me to *follow through* the life of discipleship,
    not allowing myself to become distracted,
    nor to lose heart so that I wander away from you,
    but keeping faith to the end.
Lord Jesus Christ,
    you call me,
    as you call all your people,
    to follow.

Teach me what that means,
 and by your grace help me to respond
 and to walk faithfully in your way,
 to the glory of your name.
Amen.

100
Lord,
 it's hard,
 faced with disappointment,
 to find new reserves and fresh inspiration
 to try and try again.
When I've given my all
 and believe I've achieved something,
 when I've kept on battling
 despite the obstacles in my way,
 it hurts to accept
 that there are still more hurdles to face,
 more setbacks to overcome.
Yet though I may sometimes feel weary at the demands,
 I know in my heart
 that life is made of such challenges;
 that no achievement,
 however special,
 is sufficient to answer all my dreams.
Renew me, then, through your Holy Spirit,
 and give me the faith
 and commitment I need to walk the pilgrim way,
 pressing on towards the prize you set before me.
Amen.

101
Lord Jesus Christ,
 it is not easy to follow you;
 not if I am serious about discipleship.

You challenge my whole perspective on life,
    calling me not just to a statement of belief
    but to a way of life.
You are always leading me forward,
    eager to guide me into new experiences of your love
    and a deeper understanding of your purpose,
    yet so often I refuse to follow
    where you would have me go.
Forgive me for losing the sense of direction
    that marked my early days of discipleship.
Forgive me for trusting you when all goes well
    but doubting the moment life fails
    to conform to my expectations.
Forgive me for thinking that I have done all
    that needs to be done,
    imagining that one simple confession
    of faith suffices for a lifetime.
Lord,
    you are still calling,
    inviting me to respond.
Help me to walk in your footsteps.
Amen.

102
Lord,
    you do not call me to a destination but a journey –
    a journey of continual new discoveries
    and new experiences of your love.
Save me from ever thinking I have arrived;
    from imagining I know all there is to know
    or that I have exhausted the riches of everything
    you would reveal to me.
Open my eyes to the great adventure of life
    and to the unfathomable mysteries of your purpose,
    and so help me to live as a pilgrim,

travelling in faith,
until I reach at last the kingdom
you hold in store for all your people.
Amen.

103
Loving God,
I thank you for those moments in my life
that have been milestones in my journey of faith –
moments when I have been especially conscious
of your presence,
when faith has grown,
when truth has dawned on me
in an unmistakable way.
I thank you for such times
but I pray you will help me always to recognise
that my journey is not ended
but only just begun.
Teach me that, however many answers I may have,
there is always more to see,
more to learn
and more to understand,
and so may I know you
a little more deeply each day
through Jesus Christ my Lord.
Amen.

104
Gracious God,
whenever I lose my way,
call me back and help me
to turn again to the living way,
through Jesus Christ my Lord.
Amen.

105

May the word of God guide my footsteps,
    the power of God equip me for service,
    the grace of God renew me
    and the love of God surround me always.
May Christ be my constant companion
    on the path of discipleship,
    until my journey is over
    and I meet with him face to face,
    secure in the joy of his everlasting kingdom.
In his name I ask it.
Amen.

106

Sovereign God,
    equip me with faith, hope, courage,
    resilience, enthusiasm and dedication,
    so that I may walk the path of discipleship faithfully,
    through good or ill, to the glory of your name.
Amen.

107

Lord Jesus Christ,
    help me to walk the journey
    to which you have called me,
    keeping faith in your saving purpose.
When I grow weary, revive me;
    when I go astray, direct me;
    when I lose heart, inspire me,
    and when I turn back, reprove me.
Keep me travelling ever onwards,
     trusting in your guidance and certain
    that you will be there at my journey's end
    to welcome me home into your eternal kingdom.
In your name, I ask it.
Amen.

108

Lord Jesus Christ,
    teach me to travel light and to let go of all
    that may encumber me on my journey.
So may I walk your way faithfully to the end,
    to the glory of your name.
Amen.

Cost

109

Living God,
    it is uncomfortable sometimes having to choose.
I prefer to sit on the fence,
    to hedge my bets,
    to take the path of compromise
    in the hope of pleasing all.
Even when I know the right way,
    I turn aside from it,
    fearful of the cost that may be involved.
Yet, deep down, I know this simply won't do;
    that failing to decide *for* you
    means deciding *against* you.
Help me to recognise when I need to make a choice,
    and then give me courage to stand firm in faith,
    whatever it may cost.
Amen.

110

Lord Jesus Christ,
    it is easy to talk of taking up my cross
    and following you,
    but the reality is different.
I find it hard to deny myself even a little,
    let alone to give my all.

There is so much I want to enjoy,
    so much I want to achieve,
    and the thought of sacrificing any of that
    is one I would rather push aside.
Yet you have taught that it is in losing our lives
    we truly find them,
    and that we shall find lasting treasures
    not on earth but in heaven.
Help me, then, instead of clinging slavishly
    to self-interest,
    to give of myself freely,
    just as you gave yourself for me.
Amen.

111
Lord Jesus Christ,
    faced with difficult decisions
    so often I tell myself I have no choice,
    that life has pushed me into a corner,
    leaving me no alternative as to how to act.
But in my heart I know that this isn't so.
It may be hard, painful or costly,
    but finally there is always a right way
    if I am prepared to look for it.
Forgive me for all the excuses I make.
Forgive me for the ways I wriggle and squirm
    rather than face up to my responsibilities.
Forgive me for all the times I have taken the soft option
    rather than the one I know to be right.
Teach me, next time I have to make a choice,
    to seek your will,
    to listen to your voice
    and to respond in faith,
    to the glory of your name.
Amen.

112

Gracious God,
     forgive me my mean and selfish spirit –
     my desire so often to safeguard pleasures for myself,
     to provide for my own well-being while ignoring
     the needs of others.
Teach me that it is in giving we receive,
     in denying ourselves that we discover true riches.
Help me not just to assent to this intellectually,
     but also to believe it in my heart
     and show it in my life.
Give me a heart overflowing with generosity,
     eager to share with others
     the good things you have given to me,
     and so may I add both to their joy and to my own,
     through Jesus Christ our Lord.
Amen.

113

Lord Jesus Christ,
     no one can ever give me more than you have given,
     for you have blessed me with life itself –
     life overflowing with good things,
     life eternal –
     and to make that gift possible you gave of yourself,
     not just a little but all.
You bore the limitations of human flesh;
     you endured rejection,
     humiliation
     and, finally, death on a cross;
     and,
     most awesome of all,
     you took on yourself the dreadful burden
     of this world's sinfulness,
     experiencing despair and isolation
     to make all things whole.

Forgive me that, despite all this,
   I give so grudgingly in return.
Forgive me that though my words say one thing
   my life says another;
   that my thoughts are so little for you
   and still less for others.
Help me to catch again a glimpse of the love
   you have so freely given
   and to spontaneously give of myself in return
   in joyful and heartfelt thanksgiving,
   for your name's sake.
Amen.

114

Living God,
   you spoke through Jesus of going the extra mile,
   to do more than anyone can ask or expect.
Forgive me that I find that so hard:
   that I prefer to do as little as possible
   rather than as much;
   that I give my help, time, service and money
   grudgingly rather than cheerfully.
I praise you for the readiness of Christ
   to go not just the extra mile
   but to give his all,
   identifying himself with our human condition,
   willingly experiencing suffering and death
   so that we might discover life in its fullness.
I praise you for those
   who have followed in his footsteps,
   willing to go beyond the call of duty
   in the service of others.
Touch my heart through their example
   and inspire me through the love of Christ,
   so that I may be more ready to do that little bit extra,

to go beyond people's expectations,
to give as you have given so freely.
In the name of Christ I ask it.
Amen.

115
Lord Jesus Christ,
I want to follow your example
and I strive to do so,
but so often my weakness gets the better of me.
I talk of serving others
but live instead for myself;
I speak of self-sacrifice but indulge my self-interest;
I profess loyalty to your cause,
yet repeatedly deny it through the way I live.
I have preferred my way to yours,
more concerned with my own advancement
than your kingdom.
I have been weak in my commitment
and half-hearted in offering my service.
Forgive me all the ways my life fails
to reflect your goodness
and my faithlessness betrays your grace.
Touch my life afresh
and fill my heart with your love
so that I may truly live for you,
making known your love
and bringing closer your kingdom.
In your name I ask it.
Amen.

116
Lord,
it's easy to follow you when life is going well;
much harder when I come up against problems.

Forgive me for the weakness of my faith,
    for being a fair-weather disciple,
    swift to turn back when the going gets rough.
Help me to recognise that there are times
    when I must face challenges
    and overcome apparently insurmountable obstacles,
    and teach me that you are as much with me
    in those times as at any other.
Give me courage to walk wherever you lead,
    confident that you will never forsake me.
Amen.

117

Lord Jesus Christ,
    teach me the values of your kingdom
    and the joy of knowing you,
    so that I may put you first and self second,
    to the glory of your name.
Amen.

118

Lord Jesus Christ,
    teach me to let go of self,
    to focus on the things that really matter,
    and thus to discover life in all its fullness,
    through your grace.
Amen.

119

God of justice,
    quicken my conscience and stir my heart
    so that I may show my faith
    not simply in easy words but in costly actions.
Teach me what it means to deny myself,
    and, in doing so, may I bring joy,
    help and hope to others.
Amen.

120

Living God,
    open my heart to what you would say
    even when I would rather not hear it.
Open my life to what you would have me do,
    even when I would rather not do it.
Help me to respond to your disturbing,
    challenging word,
    in the name of Christ.
Amen.

Growth

121

Living God,
    I know what my life ought to be like,
    I know what it *is* like,
    and I am ashamed at the difference between the two.
Where I ought to reveal Christ,
    I point instead to myself.
Where I ought to bear witness to his life-changing power,
    I demonstrate instead how little has actually changed.
So much about me denies rather than affirms the gospel,
    leading people to dismiss its claims
    rather than to explore them further.
Forgive me for all that is wrong
    and, by your Spirit, clothe me with joy,
    peace,
    patience,
    kindness,
    generosity,
    faithfulness,
    gentleness,
    self-control,
    and, above all, love.

Work in my life,
and through me speak to others,
through the grace of Christ.
Amen.

122

Almighty God,
through Christ you have demonstrated
the wonder of your goodness,
the awesome extent of your love.
You call me to follow in his footsteps –
to reflect through my life and witness
more of that same gracious love.
Forgive me for failing to do that –
for failing to show in my life
the faith I profess with my lips.
Forgive me that all too often the picture I give
is a feeble caricature,
a pathetic parody of the Lord I so hunger to serve.
Take, then, what I am
and, by your grace, make me what I long to be,
so that I may truly bring glory to you,
through Jesus Christ my Lord.
Amen.

123

Living God,
forgive me for being content to drift along
with little sense of direction or purpose;
for assuming it is enough to get by,
and failing to ensure that I do even that.
Give me courage to examine myself honestly,
to take stock of my life carefully and prayerfully,
to face up to truth and see myself as I am,
and glimpse what I could
and should be with your help.

Help me to tackle the things I prefer to push aside,
    pretending they are not there –
    to recognise my weaknesses as well as my strengths,
    my faults as well as my virtues.
So may I grow each day in faith
    and live more fully to your praise and glory,
    through Jesus Christ my Lord.
Amen.

124

Lord Jesus Christ,
    there is so much within me that is not as it should be:
    thoughts, attitudes, desires and fears
    that alienate me from others and from you
    and that disturb, divide and ultimately destroy.
I long to be like you:
    to feel the same love and compassion that you felt,
    to experience the same closeness with God,
    and to know the same inner wholeness and harmony.
Alone, though, I cannot achieve it,
    no amount of effort sufficient
    to help me emulate your example.
Draw closer to me through your grace,
    and fill me in body, mind and soul.
Speak to me,
    teach and guide, so that I may know you better.
Work within my heart,
    transforming the clay of my life into a new creation,
    moulded by your hands.
In your name I ask it.
Amen.

125

Living God,
    I thank you for the seed of faith
    you have sown within me

and for the way it has grown across the years,
but I confess also that there are times
when all is not as it should be.
Instead of continuing to flourish,
my commitment starts to flag and my vision to wilt,
choked by other interests and concerns,
suffocated by complacency
and starved of space in which to expand.
Forgive me for allowing that to happen
and accepting it as the norm.
Help me to open my life to you
so that you can feed me through your word,
nourish me through your Spirit
and nurture me through the gracious love of Christ,
in whose name I pray.
Amen.

126

Living God,
I turned to you once
and, naively, I imagined I had done
all that needed doing;
that from then on I would say goodbye to my old self
and live in newness of life.
The reality, I have found,
is that two selves war within me.
Help me, then, to turn to you once more,
and to go on doing so for however long it takes.
Help me, each day, to put off the old self
and to be renewed in body,
mind and spirit through your grace,
until in the fullness of time
you have finished your redemptive work
and made of me a new creation,
through Jesus Christ my Lord.
Amen.

127

Sovereign God,
   I thank you for the way you are at work in my life,
   constantly looking to refashion me in your image.
I praise you that, despite my lack of faith,
   my many faults
   and my sometimes wilful disobedience,
   you never give up,
   patiently looking to re-create me
   through the power of your Holy Spirit.
Come to me now in all my weakness,
   and by your grace,
   renew, redeem and restore me
   in the likeness of Christ,
   for his name's sake.
Amen.

128

Loving God,
   occasionally there are moments
   that I never want to end,
   moments so special
   that I wish time would stand still
   so that I could hold on to them for ever,
   but I know that life and faith are not like that,
   instead always needing to move on
   if they are not to grow stale.
Help me, then,
   to be open to new experiences of your love
   new insights into your greatness,
   new responses to your call,
   and a new awareness of your guidance,
   so that I may know you better each day,
   until I rejoice in your presence
   for all eternity,

in the joy of Christ that will never fade or perish.
In his name I ask it.
Amen.

129
Lord Jesus Christ,
    I remember your words to the disciples
    that the kingdom of heaven belongs to little children,
    and I remember also your warning
    that unless we become like children
    we can never hope to enter that kingdom.
Teach me what that means.
Grant me the childlike qualities I need to grow in faith –
    a child's innocence and hunger to learn,
    a child's love and total trust.
Help me,
    like them,
    to step out gladly into the great adventure of faith,
    to the glory of your name.
Amen.

130
Lord Jesus Christ,
    just as you brought new out of old
    through your fulfilment of the Law and the prophets,
    so also continue to make me new,
    taking my old self and refashioning it by your grace
    into a new creation.
Help me to let go of everything in my past
    that denies and destroys,
    separating me from your love.
Take what I am and re-create me by your power,
    so that I may be the person you would have me be,
    for I ask it in your name.
Amen.

131

Lord Jesus Christ,
    I am not good at letting go of the past,
    at recognising there are times
    when I need to move on in life;
    to take a step forward in faith
    if I am ever truly to grow.
I prefer the security of the familiar,
    the comfort of that which does not stretch
    or challenge me too far,
    and I am wary of the prospect of change,
    afraid that it might ask more of me
    than I am willing to give.
I am not good at letting go of the old
    and putting on the new,
    at turning away from my former way of life
    and taking instead the way of the cross.
I am reluctant to abandon old habits,
    fearful of being thought different,
    unwilling to deny myself the pleasures of this world
    for the promise of the world to come.
So I try to keep a foot in both camps,
    to combine the old self with the new.
I think I can balance the two,
    but, of course, I can't,
    and the result is that I compromise both
    and embrace neither.
Help me to understand that,
    while the old has its place,
    there are some areas in life
    where a complete break is needed,
    a turning away from what has been,
    before I am ready to receive what shall be.
Lord Jesus Christ,
    you want to work within me
    to finish the new creation you have begun.

Give me courage to trust you completely,
    so that you may refashion my life to your glory.
I ask it in your name.
Amen.

132

Loving God,
    I praise you for the way you have worked in my life:
    the way you have offered me a new beginning,
    a new identity
    and a new sense of purpose,
    constantly working within me
    to refashion and redeem me.
I thank you that, despite my weakness,
    you are able to take and use me
    far beyond my expectations.
Forgive me everything within me
    that frustrates your will,
    and, by your grace, continue to draw me to yourself,
    remaking me as a living testimony
    to your sovereign saving love,
    through Jesus Christ my Lord.
Amen.

133

God of truth,
    you know me better than I know myself.
You search my heart and mind,
    seeing me as I really am
    and confronting me with my true self.
Forgive me that all too often I shy away
    from what is hard to accept,
    refusing to countenance anything
    that contradicts my self-image.
I find it so difficult to be honest,
    closing my ears to truths I would rather not hear.

I avoid those who challenge and disturb me,
   preferring instead those who soothe
   and flatter my ego.
Thank you for those with the rare gift
   of speaking the truth in love;
   those prepared to risk my resentment,
   retaliation or rejection
   not out of spite or vindictiveness
   but because they genuinely care
   and want to help me grow as an individual.
God of all,
   give me true humility and meekness of spirit,
   so that I may be ready to listen and examine myself;
   ready to ask searching questions about who I am,
   ready to face the truth and to change where necessary.
In Christ's name I ask it.
Amen.

134

Lord Jesus Christ,
   when my faith is weak, strengthen it;
   when it is shallow, nurture it;
   when it is flawed, correct it;
   and when it is partial, complete it,
   for your name's sake.
Amen.

135

Living God,
   grant me the wisdom of years
   and the enthusiasm of childhood,
   the discernment of adulthood
   and the innocence of youth.
Help me to rediscover the child in me
   and so grow to maturity in you.
Amen.

136
Lord Jesus Christ,
    teach me that if I would live for *you*,
    you first must live in *me*.
Amen.

Faith

137

Lord Jesus Christ,
    I was not there at the stable like the shepherds;
    I was not one of the twelve who
    you chose to be your Apostles;
    I was not able to see you heal the sick;
    I was not there as you broke bread in the upper room,
    as they pressed the crown of thorns on your head,
    as you suffered on the cross,
    as you appeared to the disciples
    following your resurrection,
    as you ascended into heaven.
Yet I can know you as much as any who *were* there,
    for you are with me now,
    with me always,
    here by my side.
Lord Jesus Christ,
    I thank you for the daily reality
    of your living presence.
Amen.

138

Loving God,
    I do not know all there is to know,
    or understand all there is to understand,
    but one thing I am sure of:
    that in Jesus Christ I have met with you,
    experiencing your love,
    rejoicing in your mercy,
    receiving your guidance,
    thrilling to your blessing.
There is much still to learn
    and much that will always be beyond me,

but I have seen and heard enough
to convince me of your grace,
and I have tasted sufficient of your goodness
to know that nothing can ever separate me
from your love revealed in Christ.
Help me to serve as he taught,
to love as he urged,
and to trust as he instructed.
So may I live in him and he in me,
to the glory of your name.
Amen.

139

Gracious God,
I thank you for the many ways you provide for me,
the love you so faithfully show
and the blessings you give beyond my deserving.
Forgive me for taking your goodness for granted
instead of appreciating it as I should.
Forgive me for failing to trust you
despite all you have done,
trusting instead in other people or other things.
Teach me to put my faith in you,
knowing that whatever I may be up against
you will provide the help I need to face it,
through Jesus Christ my Lord.
Amen.

140

Loving God,
I thank you that you are a God I can depend on,
a God in whom I can put my trust.
What you promise is done;
what you purpose is fulfilled.

I remember your promise to Abraham –
    that, through his offspring,
    all the world would be blessed;
    to Moses –
    that you would lead the Israelites out of Egypt;
    to Isaiah –
    that you would deliver your people from exile;
    to your prophets –
    that the Messiah would come;
    to the Apostles –
    that he would rise again on the third day.
I thank you that you fulfilled those promises,
    just as you said you would –
    your Son born from the line of Abraham,
    your chosen nation set free from slavery,
    your people returning joyfully to Jerusalem,
    your promised deliverer born in Bethlehem,
    your power seen in the resurrection of Christ.
I thank you for what that means for me today –
    that I can live each moment with confidence,
    whatever my circumstances may be,
    whatever times of testing may befall me,
    knowing that, though all else may fail,
    you will not;
    though heaven and earth may pass away,
    your words will endure for ever.
So I look forward to that day
    when your purpose is fulfilled
    and you are all in all.
Until then, I will trust in you,
    secure in your love,
    confident in your eternal purpose,
    assured that your will shall be done.
Receive my thanks,
    in the name of Christ.
Amen.

141

Gracious God,
    I want to trust you,
    but I find it hard to do so sometimes.
I see problems rather than opportunities.
I remember failure instead of success.
I am filled with doubt rather than faith.
Like your servant Gideon, long ago,
    I crave a sign,
    some assurance that you will see me safely through.
Forgive me for finding it so difficult to rely on you,
    for so easily forgetting all you have done for me.
I do not deserve any proof,
    yet in your mercy you repeatedly provide
    evidence of your love.
Teach me to trust you without reserve,
    and grant that I may draw closer to you
    until I need no further confirmation of your purpose
    than the daily, living reality of your presence.
Amen.

142

Loving God,
    I thank you that in the turmoil of life
    you are always with me –
    your love reaching out,
    your hand supporting me
    and your grace giving me strength.
Help me truly to believe that,
    not just in my mind but also in my heart;
    to put my trust wholly in you,
    confident that you will never fail me.
Help me to let go of the fears and anxieties
    that weigh me down,
    that destroy my confidence
    and undermine my happiness,

that alienate me from others
and prevent me living life to the full.
Help me to receive the freedom you offer,
which comes from knowing
that you hold all things in your hands
and that nothing can finally separate me
from your love.
In the name of Christ I ask it.
Amen.

143
Sovereign God,
I thank you that whatever I may face,
whatever dangers may threaten me,
you are able to deliver me from evil.
In life and in death you are by my side,
nothing able to separate me
from the wonder of your love.
Help me, then, to trust you always,
to love you unswervingly
and to honour you each day
with faithful and committed service,
to the glory of your name.
Amen.

144
Loving God,
it is hard sometimes to continue believing
when so much denies my convictions.
It is harder still when those around me
ridicule my faith
and deride me for following you,
and it is hardest of all when hopes are dashed
and you seem far from me,
my prayers for help seemingly unanswered.
Give me strength,
despite adversity or disappointment,

to stay true to you,
trusting in your purpose,
in the assurance that your way will finally prevail.
Amen.

145
Lord,
it's hard to keep striving sometimes
when all my efforts meet with failure;
hard to keep praying when all my prayers
seem to be unanswered;
hard to keep believing when so much in life
seems to undermine my faith.
Yet it is at such times as those
that I need to hold firmly to you,
discovering the strength that you alone can give
and trusting in your sovereign purpose.
Teach me to persevere
even when the odds
seem hopelessly stacked against me,
confident that your will shall finally prevail
despite everything that conspires against it.
Help me to know that
though I may be tempted to give up on you,
you will never give up on me!
Amen.

146
Sovereign God,
it is easy to trust you when life is good,
but when circumstances change,
then faith is suddenly put to the test.
When one problem,
one anxiety,
one sorrow follows another,
I feel overwhelmed,

swimming against a current
that sweeps me deeper and deeper into difficulty.
Teach me that however fierce the storm,
it can never finally swamp me,
for you will be there to rescue me
in my time of need.
Teach me to hold firmly to you
knowing that you will keep hold of me
until the storm is past and calm returns.
In Jesus' name I pray.
Amen.

147

Gracious God,
when life is testing
and your purpose is hard to fathom,
help me to remember
that you are able to see me through.
When I feel overwhelmed by the challenge before me,
yet see nowhere and no one to turn to,
remind me to reach out to you,
knowing that whenever I need you,
you will be there.
Teach me that, with you,
no situation is beyond hope,
and that no darkness
can ever fully extinguish the light,
and in that confidence may I walk each day in faith,
to the glory of your name.
Amen.

148

Lord Jesus Christ,
deliver me from a flabby couch-potato faith,
so out of condition that it is doomed
finally to collapse and die.

Teach me to put faith into action,
    so that it may be stretched and grow,
    equipping me for service in your kingdom,
    through Christ my Lord.
Amen.

149

Gracious God,
    in the good and the bad, the happy and the sad,
    help me to keep on trusting you,
    confident that your purpose will win through
    and your love triumph over all.
Amen.

150

Loving God,
    I do not know what lies ahead,
    except that there will be a mixture
    of good and bad,
    joy and sorrow,
    but I know for certain that,
    in life or in death,
    you will be with me,
    waiting to enrich my life,
    to bestow your blessing
    and to fulfil your sovereign purpose.
In that faith, I commit the future to you,
    through Jesus Christ my Lord.
Amen.

151

Sovereign God,
    teach me that though much is beyond *me*,
    nothing is beyond *you*.
Amen.

152

Sovereign God,
> teach me to trust in you
> even when I cannot see the way ahead.

Help me to walk in faith,
> even when faith seems foolish.

Grant me grace to entrust myself
> to your everlasting arms,
> in the assurance that you will be sufficient
> for all my needs.

Amen.

Forgiveness

153

Sovereign God,
    I thank you that you judge not by the outside
    but by the person underneath;
    not simply by my faithless actions
    but by my underlying desire to serve you.
Where I am swift to condemn,
    you are eager to forgive.
You are always ready to show mercy,
    to believe in my potential
    rather than dwell on my past record.
Save me from interpreting your judgement
    in terms of my own narrow horizons;
    from attributing to you a strictness
    that reflects my own narrow outlook
    and that denies your grace.
Teach me to receive your forgiveness
    and to rejoice in the newness of life you long to bring,
    through Jesus Christ my Lord.
Amen.

154

Gracious God,
    I don't find it easy to give someone a second chance,
    especially when they've let me down personally.
It's hard to overcome feelings of hurt and anger,
    and harder still ever to trust that person
    in the way I used to.
Yet you go on giving me another chance day after day,
    and, despite my repeated failure,
    you are willing still to trust me
    with the work of your kingdom.
Teach me, then, instead of dwelling on faults,
    to look for strengths;

instead of putting people down,
to lift them up;
and instead of consigning them to the scrap heap,
to give them the benefit of the doubt.
Help me to forgive others as you forgive me,
in Christ's name.
Amen.

155
Gracious God,
I have no reason to expect your mercy,
for though I say I am sorry
I go on letting you down time after time,
making the same mistakes I have always made,
ignoring your will,
even wilfully rejecting your guidance.
Yet you go on forgiving me,
year in, year out,
always ready to receive me back
and to help me start again.
I praise you for the wonder of your love,
your goodness that is never exhausted.
Help me, having been forgiven so much,
to forgive others,
whose mistakes are so little by comparison.
Give me a generous heart and graciousness of spirit,
so that I do not simply speak of forgiveness
but also display the truth of it in my life,
through Jesus Christ my Lord.
Amen.

156
Gracious God,
you tell us that as we forgive so we shall be forgiven,
and the thought of that is frightening,
for I find forgiving others so very difficult.

When I am hurt,
   insulted,
   let down,
   my natural inclination is to want revenge,
   and I allow that thirst to fester within me
   until it grows out of all proportion
   to the wrong I have suffered.
Teach me to leave vengeance to you,
   knowing that in your own time justice will be done.
Amen.

157
Gracious God,
   I have so much to thank you for,
   and yet there are times when I lose sight of that,
   dwelling instead on the disappointments
   and frustrations of life.
I brood about the things that didn't work out as I hoped,
   the hurts inflicted upon me,
   the mistakes made,
   the opportunities denied,
   and I allow these to fester within me,
   poisoning me from within,
   eating away at my happiness
   until I think of nothing else.
Forgive my foolishness
   and help me to regain a proper sense of proportion.
Teach me to put the past behind me
   and to embrace the present moment,
   recognising that what's done is done
   but that you are constantly making all things new.
Save me from that sourness of spirit
   that accomplishes nothing
   and that finally will serve only to destroy me.
In Christ's name I pray.
Amen.

158
Lord Jesus Christ,
  the Way, the Truth and the Life,
  forgive me the times I have kept you out of my life,
  preferring to do my own thing in my own way
  and believing I have no need of your help.
Forgive me the times
  I have kept you standing on the doorstep,
  not wanting to face your challenge
  or to have my comfortable lifestyle
  questioned by the truth.
Forgive me the times I have welcomed you for a moment
  only to show you the door later,
  faith proving incompatible or hard to reconcile
  with certain aspects of my life.
Help me to open the door of my heart without reserve
  and to keep it open, come what may.
Come now and make your home in me
  so that I may dwell in you always,
  rejoicing in your love
  and celebrating your glorious gift of new life.
Amen.

159
Gracious God,
  give me the wisdom and humility I need
  to recognise my mistakes,
  to acknowledge them openly,
  to seek forgiveness, and, where possible,
  to make amends.
Amen.

160
Sovereign God,
  when I do wrong,
  give me courage to acknowledge it

before you and others,
so that I may know your forgiveness
and open a way to the healing of the wounds
my mistakes have caused.
Amen.

161
Lord Jesus Christ,
touch my life with your healing forgiveness,
and put a new heart and a right spirit within me,
so that I may truly love you and faithfully serve you,
to the glory of your name.
Amen.

God

God's Call

162

Sovereign God,
> you spoke and the universe was created:
> the heavens and the earth,
> the night and day,
> the sea and dry land –
> life in all its bewildering variety and beauty.

You spoke again,
> and your people heard your voice –
> Abraham, Isaac and Jacob,
> Moses, Joshua, Elijah,
> kings, priests, judges, prophets –
> an ever-growing succession
> of those who listened to your word
> and responded to your call.

You spoke in Christ,
> your call coming once more –
> to shepherds and magi,
> tax-collectors and sinners,
> rich and poor,
> men and women –
> your word bringing light and hope,
> joy and life.

You speak still –
> to me as much as any –
> offering your mercy, wholeness and renewal,
> but calling also to loving service and bold witness.

Help me, like those who have gone before,
> to respond in faith,
> ready to follow where you will lead,
> working for the growth of your kingdom
> and the glory of your name.

In the name of Christ I pray.
Amen.

163
Loving God,
   I thank you for your call:
   to discipleship, fellowship and service;
   to sharing with your people
   in the work of your kingdom.
I thank you that you call me as I am,
   with all my faults, weaknesses and doubts,
   accepting me not through my own deserving,
   but through your grace,
   your love,
   and your mercy.
Above all, I thank you for the inner presence
   of your Holy Spirit,
   through which Christ is constantly
   at work within me,
   moving deep within to change my life
   and to draw me ever closer to you.
Loving God,
   receive my praise in his name.
Amen.

164
Loving God,
   forgive me for refusing sometimes
   to listen to your voice.
Deep down in my heart of hearts
   I know you are speaking to me,
   but I would rather not hear.
When your message is too demanding,
   when you ask of me what I would rather not face,
   when your words make me feel uncomfortable,

striking too near the mark,
I stubbornly resist,
closing my ears and pushing you away.
Yet however hard I may try,
I will never finally silence your voice –
not until I have listened and responded.
Help me, then, to hear what you would say to me,
and act upon it.
Amen.

165
Loving God,
there are times when,
no matter how I call,
you seem silent,
when I cannot hear your voice
no matter how I listen for it.
Grant me courage in those moments
to ask if I have closed my heart and mind
to what you would say,
but help me also to understand that there are times
when you expect me
to get on with the business of discipleship
without you directing my every step.
Help me to see that your silence
need not be a sign of my faithlessness
or of your displeasure,
but might rather point to your love,
offering me the opportunity
to grow towards Christian maturity.
Help me, then, to remember
all those times you have spoken unmistakably,
and let those moments sustain and direct me
until your word comes again,
through Jesus Christ.
Amen.

166

Gracious God,

    you speak to me in all kinds of ways,

    through all kinds of people;

    forgive me that I am sometimes closed

    to what you have to say.

I avoid that which challenges, disturbs or unsettles me,

    preferring to criticise and condemn

    rather than face the issues raised.

Forgive me that I shut my ears

    to what I don't agree with,

    rather than listen to another point of view;

    that I am reluctant to accept new and unfamiliar ideas,

    taking refuge instead in what is tried and trusted.

Forgive me that I can become so bogged down

    in what I think is right,

    so sure of my own convictions and set in my ways

    that I resent anything different.

Open my heart to the living reality of Christ,

    my mind to the sweeping breath of your Holy Spirit,

    and my soul to all that you would do and say.

Amen.

167

Living God,

    teach me to hear your cry in the groans of the hungry,

    the suffering of the sick,

    the plight of the homeless

    and the sorrow of the bereaved;

    to hear your call in the misery of the lonely,

    the despair of the oppressed,

    the plea of the weak

    and the helplessness of the poor.

Teach me to listen and to respond,

    in the name of Christ.

Amen.

168
Loving God,
    there are times in my life
    when you call me to tasks that seem beyond me,
    tasks I would rather avoid.
I hear your voice but feel unable to meet the challenge
    and my natural inclination is to run away.
Remind me that when you ask me to do something,
    you give me the strength I need to do it.
Give me courage, then, to respond when you call,
    knowing that, however things may seem,
    you are always able to transform them
    in ways far beyond my expectations.
Amen.

169
Gracious God,
    when I listen for your voice,
    save me from deciding what I want you to say
    before you have a chance to speak.
Amen.

170
Loving God,
    draw close to me
    and help me to draw nearer to you.
Speak to me and help me to hear.
Challenge me and help me to respond.
Enthuse me with the wonder of your love,
    and so may joy and peace fill my heart,
    now and for evermore.
Amen.

171
Living God, whatever you call me to do,
    help me to perform it faithfully,

gladly and wholeheartedly,
to the glory of your name.
Amen.

God's Faithfulness

172
Almighty God,
    I remember again all you have done across the years:
    your creative acts,
    your mighty deeds throughout history,
    your gift of Jesus Christ.
I remember all you have done for me:
    your sovereign love,
    your gracious mercy
    and your constant guidance every day of my life.
Forgive me that so often
    and so easily I forget those things,
    brooding instead over my troubles,
    coveting what I do not have,
    preoccupied with my personal well-being
    rather than your kingdom.
Help me each day to remind myself of your goodness,
    to recall the ways you have blessed me,
    and to keep you at the forefront of my life,
    living and working for your glory.
In Christ's name I ask it.
Amen.

173
Gracious God,
    I thank you that you are here by my side,
    wanting to meet me,
    greet me
    and teach me.
I thank you for being with me everywhere –
    at every moment,

every place and every occasion –
watching over me as a father watches over his child.
Day by day,
    you stay close –
    recognised or unrecognised,
    remembered or forgotten,
    obeyed or disobeyed,
    acknowledged or taken for granted.
Though my response to you is varied
    and my commitment wavering,
    you are always the same:
    ever-faithful,
    all-loving,
    always true.
I have no way of knowing what the future may hold,
    whether for good or ill,
    but what I do know,
    and hold on to,
    is that you will remain the same,
    always there when I need you,
    nothing finally able to separate me
    from your love in Christ.
For that assurance,
    receive my praise,
    in his name.
Amen.

174
Living God,
    help me to remember that you are a God
    who never sleeps,
    a God on whom I can depend
    in any and every situation.
When I feel lost and alone,
    teach me that you are there.

When I feel overwhelmed by trouble,
  unsure of my ability to get through,
  help me to remember that you are close by.
When I feel uncertain of the way ahead,
  fearful of what the future may hold,
  teach me that you are watching over me.
Help me to understand that, whatever I may face,
  you will guide and guard me,
  protecting me from evil
  and enfolding me in your everlasting arms,
  and in that knowledge
  may I meet every day with quiet trust
  and glad thanksgiving,
  in Christ's name.
Amen.

175
Loving God,
  I know I shouldn't be afraid, but sometimes I am –
  afraid of what the future might hold
  and whether I will have the strength to meet it.
Thank you for the assurance that whatever I may face,
  you will be there beside me.
Thank you for your promise to lift me up
  and help me to start again,
  however often I may fail.
Thank you for the times
  you have reached out in the past,
  the experiences I can look back on
  when your arms have been there to support me
  when I needed them most.
Teach me to trust you more completely
  and to step out in faith,
  confident that, though I may stumble,
  you will set me on my feet once more.
Amen.

176
Lord,
   even when I cannot see you,
   when life seems dark and hope seems to be in vain,
   teach me to keep faith with you,
   knowing that you will keep faith with me.
Amen.

God's Grace

177
Living God,
   I thank you for your amazing grace,
   your love of me as I am,
   despite all my faults and weaknesses.
I praise you that you accept me
   not through my own efforts
   or according to my own deserving,
   but through faith in Christ.
Forgive me for abusing that truth sometimes,
   throwing your love back into your face
   through taking it for granted.
Forgive me for assuming sometimes
   I can carry on regardless,
   secure in the knowledge of your mercy.
Give me a longing to serve you better
   and to grow in the likeness of Christ,
   not in any attempt to justify myself
   but simply to express my love for you.
Fill me now with your Spirit,
   and so help me to live each day in newness of life,
   to the glory of your name.
Amen.

178
Almighty God,
   I have no claim on your love,

no reason to feel I deserve it,
for I am false and faithless in so much,
but I want to know and serve you better,
to glimpse your glory,
understand your greatness
and receive your blessing.
I want to taste more of your goodness
experience more of your grace
and understand more of your purpose,
and so I come,
resolved to take hold of the new life
you have promised.
Respond to me, I pray,
and, as I have come to you,
so come to me,
through Jesus Christ my Lord.
Amen.

179

Gracious God,
I thank you for the awesomeness of your love
and the wonder of your grace.
Day after day,
you show me mercy,
accepting my feeble faith and hesitant discipleship,
understanding my weakness,
putting my faults behind me
and helping me to start again.
However much I fail you,
your patience is never exhausted,
your love refuses to be denied.
I deserve so little,
yet you give so much;
my love is so weak,
yet you respond so richly;
my faith is so small,
yet you bless me so constantly.

Gracious God,
    if you dealt with me according to my deserving
    I could not hope to escape punishment,
    for I have failed you in ways too many to number,
    but your grace is greater than I can begin to imagine.
For your love that embraces all,
    and continues for eternity,
    I praise you,
    in the name of Christ.
Amen.

180
Lord Jesus Christ,
    whenever I question my worth,
    teach me that you believe in me totally,
    enough even to die for me
    so that I might enter into your kingdom,
    and in that knowledge may I live each day,
    at one with myself
    and at one with you.
Amen.

181
Sovereign God,
    I owe you everything,
    yet, by your grace,
    I owe you nothing!
Great is your name
    and greatly to be praised!
Amen.

God's Greatness

182
Eternal God,
    mighty and mysterious,
    sovereign over all,

it is beyond the power of human words
   to express your greatness,
   for you are higher than I can ever begin to imagine.
I praise you for that truth,
   yet I confess, also, that it can be hard to live with,
   for it can make you seem remote,
   distant,
   detached from my situation,
   oblivious to my need.
I thank you that such times are rare,
   but they do come –
   times when you seem so mysterious,
   so far removed from my situation,
   that I question whether you are there at all.
I seek,
   yet I do not find;
   I ask,
   but I do not receive;
   I cry out for help,
   but you do not answer.
Help me in such moments
   to gain inspiration from those who have felt
   the same before me,
   yet who have emerged from the darkness
   to find that you have been there all along,
   leading them by the hand
   even when they could not see it.
Assure me of your continuing purpose,
   your enduring love and your final triumph,
   through Jesus Christ my Lord.
Amen.

183
Gracious God,
   you are above all,
   beneath all,

beyond all,
within all.
You are God of past, present and future;
of space and time,
heaven and earth;
of all people, all creatures and all creation.
Forgive me for sometimes losing sight
of those awesome realities,
settling instead for a fragmented picture
of who you are, shaped by my narrow horizons
and my flawed and limited understanding.
Stir my imagination,
and help me to see a little more clearly each day
the wonder of your glory.
In Christ's name I ask it.
Amen.

184

Sovereign God,
all too often I lose sight of your greatness,
settling instead for a picture of you
I feel comfortable with.
I have frustrated your will
through the smallness of my vision.
I have missed opportunities to serve you
through the narrowness of my horizons.
I have denied myself your mercy
through the confines I place upon your grace.
Repeatedly I have presumed that my ways are your ways
and my thoughts your thoughts,
forgetting that you are beyond words
or human understanding.
Forgive me,
and teach me never to underestimate
the awesomeness of your being
or the extent of your love.
Amen.

185
Loving God,
   I thank you for all there is to explore
   in this wonderful world
   and fascinating universe you have given us.
I thank you for all those whose study and research
   have unlocked so many of the secrets
   concerning the origins and development of life,
   and I thank you that you have given me a mind
   with which to think, enquire and learn.
Teach me to apply myself to gaining understanding,
   but teach me also that, however much I may learn,
   true wisdom concerning ultimate realities
   lies not in human ingenuity,
   but in you,
   the beginning and end of all.
Amen.

God's Guidance

186
Living God,
   time and again I ask you to speak to me,
   to reveal your will and give me your guidance,
   but all too often when your call comes
   I fail to recognise it.
Though I talk of prayer being a two-way encounter,
   the reality is usually different;
   I seldom seriously expect to hear your voice.
Give me a readiness to listen and learn,
   so that, however you speak, I may recognise your voice
   and understand what you are saying.
Amen.

187
Living God,
   you do not compel me to serve you
   but you invite me rather to respond to your love.

You do not impose your will upon me
   or dictate the course I should take,
   but instead you offer your guidance,
   giving me signposts to walk by,
   yet ultimately leaving the decisions
   I must make in my hands.
I thank you for this wonderful expression of trust,
   this freedom to choose and discover for myself,
   and I ask that you will help me to use it wisely,
   trusting you in return,
   and seeking, so far as I understand it,
   to honour your will.
Give me wisdom and courage
   to make the right decisions,
   at the right time
   and in the right place,
   to the glory of your name.
Amen.

188
Sovereign God,
   I cannot always make sense of life.
Your purpose sometimes seems hard to understand
   and my experiences a puzzle.
I feel frustrated when things don't work out as I hope;
   confused when the way I thought
   you were leading me no longer feels right.
I am troubled when doors that once looked inviting
   suddenly seem closed firmly in my face.
I cannot be sure whether such moments
   are meant to happen
   or whether they run counter to your purpose,
   but what I know for certain
   is that where one door closes
   you are able to open another.

Help me, instead of regretting what has been,
    to look forward to what is to come
    and to be ready to grasp the future,
    responding to each opportunity
    you give me as it comes.
In the name of Christ I ask it.
Amen.

189

Gracious God,
    when I am uncertain of the way ahead,
    give me guidance, and when I feel discouraged,
    give me fresh inspiration.
May the knowledge of your unfailing love
    give me confidence that,
    whatever problems I might face
    and whatever sorrows might befall me,
    I shall still find reason to believe
    in the future you hold in store.
Amen.

God's Love

190

Lord Jesus Christ,
    like so many others I yield to pressures to conform
    in my yearning for acceptance.
I wear a socially acceptable mask,
    say the right words
    and do what's expected of me
    rather than risk rejection,
    even when it means pretending to be what I am not.
I am so used to acceptance being conditional
    that I find it hard
    not to approach you in the same way,
    feeling that I must measure up to some yardstick
    of what is pleasing to you.

Teach me that your love is not like that.
Help me to recognise that even when I fail you,
    your love is not withdrawn.
May the knowledge that you accept me as I am
    help me each day to become more fully
    the person I can be,
    through your saving grace.
Amen.

191
Lord Jesus Christ,
    before I ever loved you, you loved me;
    before I ever looked for you,
    you were seeking me out;
    before I ever made a response,
    you were guiding my footsteps.
Always you have been there taking the initiative,
    just as you did throughout your ministry
    and even at the time of your death.
In love you offered your life,
    and in love you continue to reach out,
    never resting until the journey of discipleship is over
    and the race is won.
To you be praise and glory,
    honour and thanksgiving,
    now and for evermore.
Amen.

192
Gracious God,
    I do not find it easy to love myself,
    despite the way it may seem.
I find it hard not to dwell on my weaknesses
    rather than my strengths,
    not to brood about mistakes and failures
    rather than rejoice in the things I have achieved.

I look at myself
   and I see the faults and ugliness
   that I try to hide from the world,
   and I find the reality too painful to contemplate,
   so I try to push it away once more.
Gracious God,
   I thank you that you love me despite all this,
   that you value me not for what I might become
   but for what I am.
Teach me to live each day
   in the light of the incredible yet wonderful truth
   that you love me completely
   and want me to be at one with myself,
   through Jesus Christ my Lord.
Amen.

193
Gracious God,
   I praise you that, above all else,
   you are a God of love –
   not of judgement, anger or vengeance,
   but of constant and total love.
Though I repeatedly fail you,
   turning my back on your goodness,
   still you continue to love me,
   fiercely and wholeheartedly.
Though I turn away from you,
   wilfully rejecting your guidance
   and repeatedly betraying your trust,
   still you long to take me back,
   to restore a living, loving relationship with you.
For this awesome love,
   greater than words can express,
   deeper than I can begin to understand
   and more passionate than anything else

I shall ever experience,
I give you my thanks and offer my worship,
in the name of Christ.
Amen.

194

Lord Jesus Christ,
  you came to our world as light in its darkness.
You came out of love,
  bringing life, hope and forgiveness.
You came not to condemn but to save,
  not to judge but to show mercy.
You came willingly enduring darkness:
  the darkness of loneliness and rejection,
  of betrayal and denial,
  of suffering and humiliation,
  of fear and death,
  of all our human sinfulness
  carried on your shoulders.
Lord Jesus Christ,
  I thank you,
  I praise you,
  and I worship you.
Amen.

195

Gracious God,
  I marvel that you can love people like me,
  for there is so little about me that deserves it.
I look into the mirror of my soul
  and I am ashamed of what I see there,
  for the image is marred by greed,
  pride, selfishness, envy
  and so much else that destroys
  not just others but myself too.

Yet, incredibly, you value me to the point
that I am precious in your sight,
special enough even to die for.
If *you* can accept me, despite everything,
teach *me* to do the same
and, in learning to love myself as you do,
help me also to love others and love you,
through Jesus Christ my Lord.
Amen.

196
Gracious God,
I thank you for loving me before I ever loved you,
and for continuing to love me
even when I find it hard to love myself.
Teach me to accept what I am
and so to grow into what I can become.
Amen.

197
Gracious God,
teach me that before I can give anything,
I need first to receive,
and so open my life to your saving,
renewing love,
through Christ my Lord.
Amen.

198
Lord Jesus Christ,
show me those areas of my life
that are closed to your love,
and help me to open them fully to you,
so that you may live in me and work through me,
to the glory of your name.
Amen.

God's Purpose

199

Living God,
   I do not find it easy to live by faith.
I want some idea of what the future holds,
   some assurance that things will work out as I hope.
I like to feel in control of my life,
   able to shape events and influence my circumstances.
Above all, I feel the need to plan,
   to make provisions for myself and my loved ones,
   to map out some kind of direction for my life.
   so that I may make wise decisions for the future.
Yet my hold on life is so tenuous,
   what seems certain today under threat tomorrow,
   what seems mine one moment
   plucked from my grasp the next.
Help me, then, as I look ahead,
   to seek your guidance in all decisions,
   but teach me also to recognise
   that the future is ultimately in your hands,
   and so help me to seek your will before all else
   and to trust that, whatever life, or death, may bring,
   you will lead me safely through.
In Christ's name I ask it.
Amen.

200

Living God,
   I praise you for the assurance that your will
   shall be done and your purpose shall finally triumph.
I thank you that in all the changing circumstances of life
   you are constantly active,
   day by day working to fulfil your sovereign purpose.
Teach me, then,
   to live each moment with total confidence,

knowing that, though all else may fail,
   you will not.
Teach me to leave all things in your hands,
   secure in your love,
   convinced of your faithfulness,
   and certain that what you have promised,
   you will deliver,
   through Jesus Christ my Lord.
Amen.

201
Sovereign God,
   Lord of past, present and future,
   I thank you that in all the uncertainties of life
   I find in you one who is unchanging:
   a rock on which I can base my life,
   a fortress to protect me in times of danger
   and a shield to defend me in the journey of life.
I praise you that nothing
   can ever overcome your purpose;
   that whatever may fight against you,
   your will shall finally triumph.
In that assurance may I face each day,
   confident that you will deliver me from evil
   and lead me safely through into your eternal kingdom,
   through Jesus Christ my Lord.
Amen.

202
Sovereign God,
   I can't help wondering sometimes
   about the fairness of life.
When I see the good suffer and the wicked prosper,
   my faith is shaken and I inevitably start to question.
There is so much that doesn't seem to make sense;
   so much that appears to deny everything
   I believe about you.

Teach me, despite the apparent contradictions of life,
  to keep faith that you are there,
  striving against everything that frustrates your will
  and denies your love.
Teach me to hold on to those moments
  when I see wrongs righted and justice done.
Above all, teach me to look at the cross of Christ
  and to draw strength from the victory you won there
  over what had seemed to be the triumph of evil.
Amen.

203
Sovereign God,
  I rejoice in the knowledge that you are not distant
  from my situation,
  removed from my daily experience,
  but here by my side,
  present every moment of every day
  and intimately involved in the routine business of life,
  sharing my joys and sorrows,
  hopes and fears,
  successes and disappointments,
  pleasure and pain.
I thank you that you care about my needs,
  and are always looking to respond –
  eager to support,
  strengthen,
  comfort
  and encourage;
  to touch each moment with your grace.
Help me,
  recognising your great faithfulness,
  to consecrate every part of life into your sure keeping,
  confident that, whatever the future may hold

you will give me strength to meet it
and see me safely through.
In Christ's name I pray.
Amen.

Hope and despair

204
Loving God,
   I thank you for all those times
   when you have come to my aid,
   just when I have begun to lose hope.
I face problems and difficulties
   to which I see no solution,
   only for you to give me guidance when I need it most.
I feel hopelessly alone,
   only to discover you by my side.
I wrestle with sorrow and despair,
   only for your light to break into the darkness,
   bringing joy and hope
   through the knowledge of your love.
Teach me, through such experiences,
   to remember that, however bleak a moment may seem,
   you will never abandon or forsake me,
   and in that confidence may I live each day.
Amen.

205
Father God,
   so often in life I find that after joy comes sorrow,
   after laughter, tears,
   after pleasure, pain.
Deep down I know that I cannot have one
   without the other.
But sometimes when life is dark
   I find that hard to accept,
   even wishing I experienced no joy at all
   if it would save me pain afterwards.
Yet you were present equally, Father,
   in the joy of Jesus' birth
   and the sorrow of his death.

Teach me, then, to live with both the good
    and the bad,
    the times of celebration
    and the times of despair,
    realising that, though I may not see it,
    you are present in each of them,
    working to bring about new beginnings,
    new hope,
    whether in this life or the life to come.
In the name of Christ, I praise you.
Amen.

206

Gracious God,
    I thank you that you are always with me,
    in the bad times as well as the good,
    the difficult as well as the easy,
    the sad as well as the happy.
I thank you that though I have sometimes been
    unsure of the way ahead,
    you have always been there to guide me;
    though I have felt discouraged,
    you have offered me fresh inspiration;
    though I have been in despair,
    yet you have given me hope.
Through all the changing circumstances of life,
    I have found from personal experience
    that your steadfast love never ceases
    and that your mercies are new every morning.
May the knowledge of all you have done
    give me confidence in the days ahead,
    so that whatever problems I may face,
    whatever disappointments I may experience,
    whatever sorrows may befall me,
    I will still find reason to look forward,
    reason to believe in the future
    and reason to hope.

Lord of all hopefulness,
   hear my prayer,
   in the name of Christ.
Amen.

207
Living God,
   I praise you for the promise
   that nothing can ever overcome your light.
I thank you that even when life seems dark and hopeless,
   when I search but cannot glimpse your presence
   and call yet cannot hear your voice,
   still you are with me,
   the fire of your love inexorably burning off the clouds
   until the sun breaks through once again,
   bathing me in its light.
May that knowledge sustain me
   through the bleakest moments,
   bringing the assurance that
   good will triumph over evil,
   hope replace despair,
   joy come after sorrow,
   and life triumph over death –
   even the darkest night turned to day.
All this I ask through Jesus Christ my Lord.
Amen.

208
Lord,
   it is hard sometimes not to lose faith in your purpose.
When hopes are dashed,
   when dreams are shattered,
   when one disappointment piles up on another,
   it's difficult not to lose heart completely,
   not to retreat into a shell of despair.
I want to believe things can change,
   but there seems little evidence to support it.

I want to believe the world can be different,
 but experience appears to prove otherwise.
My heart tells me one thing,
 my head says another,
 and the latter usually wins the day.
Yet you have promised that nothing
 in heaven or on earth
 will finally overcome your purpose,
 and throughout history
 you have shown that to be true,
 constantly overturning human expectations,
 hope returning like a phoenix from the ashes.
Speak to me now through the faith
 and vision of those who have gone before me,
 so that, however dark the world may seem,
 I too may dare to hope in turn,
 through Jesus Christ my Lord.
Amen.

209
Loving God,
 so many things in life have promised much
 but delivered little.
I have set myself targets but failed to hit them.
I have achieved goals only to find
 they did not yield the satisfaction I expected.
I have been let down by others
 and, worse still, I have let myself down
 on more occasions than I care to remember.
So often, hope ends in disappointment,
 exposed as wistful naivety,
 misguided ambition or sheer foolishness.
Teach me, before all else, to trust in you,
 confident that your love
 will never fail or disappoint me.

Teach me to base my life on your living word
    that promises so much
    yet delivers even more
    than we can ever ask or imagine.
In Christ's name.
Amen.

210

Gracious God,
    you came to our world through Jesus Christ,
    and, despite everything that conspires against you,
    your love continues to shine through him.
You conquered the forces of evil,
    you overcame the sting of death,
    and you brought joy out of sorrow,
    hope out of despair.
Teach me, whatever I may face,
    to hold on to that truth,
    confident that you will always lead me
    out of darkness
    into your marvellous light.
Hold on to me when life is hard,
    and assure me that you are present
    even in the bleakest moments,
    able to use every moment of each day
    in ways beyond my imagining.
Amen.

211

Living God,
    there are times when I find it hard
    to make sense of life
    and when your purpose is difficult to fathom.
I am puzzled by my experiences,
    confused by so much that seems to contradict
    your will and deny your love,

and I wonder why you seem so distant,
so unconcerned about my needs.
Yet experience has taught me
that you are often at work in ways I do not recognise,
responding to my cry and guiding my steps,
even though I have no inkling of it at the time.
You have been with me in the darkest moments,
holding on to me even when I do not see your hand.
May that truth inspire me
whenever life proves testing,
so that, however distant you may seem,
I will know that you are near,
and stride out in that confidence.
Amen.

212
Gracious God,
when the world seems bleak and all seems lost,
remind me that through the agony
and desolation of the cross,
you were supremely at work
bringing light out of darkness,
hope out of despair,
good out of evil
and life out of death.
So help me to look to the future with faith
and to face the present at peace.
Amen.

213
Living God,
when life is hard and sorrows are many,
lead me safely through the valley of tears
until the horizon opens,
the clouds lift
and the sun shines once more.
Amen.

214
Gracious God,
 when tears are my food day and night,
 and when my heart is breaking within me,
 assure me of your love,
 reach out with your comfort,
 and help me to know that joy will come again.
Amen.

215
Lord Jesus Christ,
 as you stilled the storm
 so calm the turmoil within me.
Put my mind at rest and my spirit at peace,
 secure in the knowledge of your never-failing love.
Amen.

216
Lord Jesus Christ,
 reach out into my broken life,
 and bring joy where there is sorrow,
 healing where there is hurt,
 hope where there is despair
 and peace where there is turmoil.
In your name I pray.
Amen.

217
Gracious God,
 teach me to use even the dark moments of life
 to your glory,
 comforting others with the comfort
 I have found in you
 and staying close to them
 in their need

as you have so faithfully
stayed close to me.
In Jesus' name I pray.
Amen.

_____ Intercessions _____

218

Gracious God,
   I bring to you this broken world,
   racked by injustice and exploitation,
   suffering and sorrow,
   hatred and division –
   so few signs of hope,
   so much that invites despair.
I pray for those who work for change;
   all who strive to bring help and healing,
   hope and wholeness.
I pray for those who have stopped believing
   things can change:
   all who have lost faith in themselves,
   in others,
   in life
   or in you.
Gracious God,
   bring healing and renewal;
   finish your new creation among us.
May your will be done and your kingdom come,
   through Jesus Christ our Lord.
Amen.

219

Lord of all,
   hear the cry of the oppressed and exploited,
   the hungry and homeless,
   the sick and suffering,
   and help me to hear it too
   and to respond in your name.
Amen.

The Poor

220

Gracious God,
    I have enough and more than enough,
    but I know there are many deprived of
    even the basic necessities of life:
    who go hungry while I eat my fill;
    who have nothing to drink or wear,
    no place to call their home,
    no access to medicine or hospital care
    and no opportunity to improve their lot.
Teach me not only to pray for them
    but to respond to their plight
    by giving generously from my plenty,
    in Christ's name.
Amen.

221

Gracious God,
    I long for the day when your world
    will be as you want it to be:
    a world in which you will lift up the lowly
    and fill the hungry with good things;
    in which love and justice shall triumph,
    evil be ended
    and the meek inherit the earth.
Give me confidence that such a day will come,
    and, more than that,
    give me the resolve to help make it happen.
Help me to respond as best I can
    to the many millions who cry out for help,
    and so to play my part in bringing the dawn
    of your kingdom closer
    and turning vision into reality.
In Christ's name I ask it.
Amen.

222
Living God,
    respond to the cry of the poor
    and the entreaties of the needy,
    and grant that the time will come
    when people everywhere receive a fair reward
    for their labours, sufficient for all their needs;
    a time when this world's resources
    will be distributed justly,
    all having enough and none too much.
Amen.

The Lonely

223
Loving God,
    we pray for all who are lonely:
    those whose relationships have been broken
    or who have never enjoyed the relationships
    they might have had;
    those who feel rejected by society
    and unsure of their worth;
    those who spend day after day alone
    and those who feel hopelessly isolated
    even when they are in company.
Give to each one the knowledge
    that you are with them always,
    and help me to befriend them in turn,
    sharing the companionship I have found in you.
In the name of Christ I ask it.
Amen.

224
Lord Jesus Christ,
    may all those who feel isolated and unloved
    find in you a friend they can depend on,

and through realising how much you value them,
may they discover a sense of worth
that sustains and deepens
their relationships with others.
Amen.

The Homeless

225

Lord Jesus Christ,
  you know what it is to have nowhere
  to lay your head.
Hear then my prayer for those who are homeless,
  who live as refugees or who are forced to live
  in makeshift and inadequate housing.
Support the work of all who campaign on their behalf
  and challenge the consciences of those in authority
  so that they may do all in their power to provide
  somewhere for everyone to call their home.
Amen.

The Sick

226

Loving God,
  I bring before you the sick and suffering of this world.
I pray for those afflicted in body:
  racked by physical pain,
  wrestling with disease,
  enduring painful surgery,
  or coming to terms with terminal illness.
I pray for those disturbed or troubled in mind:
  those whose confidence has been crushed,
  no longer able to cope
  with the pressures of daily life,

oppressed by false terrors of the imagination
or facing the dark despair of depression.
I pray for those afflicted in spirit:
all who feel their lives are empty,
or whose beliefs are threatened,
or who have lost their faith
or who have become caught up in superstition,
black magic or the occult.
Living God,
reach out through all who work
to bring wholeness and healing.
Support and strengthen them in their work.
Grant them wisdom and guidance,
strength and support,
and the ability to minister something of your care
and compassion for all.
In the name of Christ I ask it.
Amen.

227
Lord Jesus Christ,
as you touched those with leprosy,
restored sight to the blind,
brought peace to the disturbed
and enabled the lame to walk,
come now to all who are sick in body,
mind and spirit.
Bring to them your healing touch and renewing grace.
Amen.

The Disabled

228
Living God,
when limitations or disabilities
make life especially hard,

remind me that you love and value all,
not for what we do, but for who we are,
and may that knowledge teach me to appreciate
and respect the worth of everyone I meet.
Amen.

The Sorrowful

229

God of all comfort,
 I bring you this world of so much pain:
 my own and that of those around me.
I bring you my hurts, troubles, anxieties and fears,
 placing them into your hands,
 and I pray for those countless others
 facing sorrow or suffering –
 hopes dashed,
 dreams broken,
 let down by those they counted dear;
 betrayed,
 abused,
 wrestling with depression or illness,
 mourning loved ones.
Hold on to us and to all who
 walk through the valley of tears.
Reach out and grant the knowledge
 that you are present, even there,
 sharing our pain and moved by our sorrow.
Minister the consolation that you alone can offer,
 and give the assurance
 that those who mourn will be comforted
 and those who weep will laugh.
Lord,
 in your mercy,
 hear my prayer,
 in Christ's name.
Amen.

230
Loving God,
   I remember today all who mourn,
   their hearts broken by tragedy,
   tears a constant companion,
   laughter and happiness seeming a distant memory.
Reach out into their pain,
   heartache and sadness,
   and give them the knowledge that you understand
   their pain and share their sorrow.
May your arms enfold them,
   your love bring comfort,
   and your light scatter the shadows,
   so that they may know joy once more
   and celebrate life in all its fullness.
Amen.

The Heavy Laden

231
Loving God,
   I pray for all who are bearing heavy burdens –
   those facing difficulties and problems
   to which they can see no solutions,
   wrestling with inner fears and phobias,
   racked by anxiety for themselves or loved ones,
   troubled about money,
   health, work
   or relationships –
   all who crave rest for their souls but cannot find it.
I pray for them and for myself,
   acknowledging that sometimes I too
   feel crushed under a weight of care.
Speak in your still small voice,
   and grant the peace and quiet confidence
   that only you can bring;
   and so may burdens be lifted and souls refreshed.
Amen.

The Dying

232

Eternal God,

    I pray for those faced by the prospect of death,
    whether wrestling with terminal illness
    or coming to terms with failing health
    and advancing years.

In all the fear and sorrow they may feel,

    give the assurance that not even death itself
    can separate them from your love;
    that you hold in store for them things more
    wonderful than they have yet begun to imagine,
    through Jesus Christ, the Lord of all.

Amen.

Workers for Justice

233

Loving God,

    hear my prayers for all who seek
    to further your will here on earth:
    those who work for peace,
    who campaign for justice,
    who strive to relieve poverty,
    who fight for the hungry –
    all who struggle for the oppressed,
    the exploited and the under-privileged.

Prosper their efforts

    and grant them inspiration
    so that they may challenge people everywhere
    to give of themselves in the service of others.

God of justice and mercy,

    hear my prayer.

Amen.

The Judicial System

234

Lord of all
   I pray for those who serve
   within the judicial system –
   barristers,
   lawyers,
   judges,
   magistrates,
   jurors
   and court officials –
   all those whose responsibility it is
   to see that justice is administered fairly to all.
Give them wisdom,
   integrity,
   courage
   and dedication,
   so that they may discharge their duties faithfully.
I pray for the police
   and all involved in the prevention
   or detection of crime,
   and for those who work in prisons,
   young offenders' institutions,
   the probation or community services
   or rehabilitation schemes.
Grant them help,
   guidance,
   strength
   and protection.
Lord of all,
   hear my prayer,
   through Jesus Christ our Lord.
Amen.

The Weak in Faith

235

Living God,
  I pray for those who find faith hard,
  those who want to believe
  but cannot get past their doubts.
I pray for those whose faith is wavering,
  undermined by the pressures and temptations of life.
I pray for those who have lost their faith,
  the fire that once burned within them extinguished.
I pray for myself,
  conscious that for me too
  faith can sometimes lose its spark.
For all those whose faith is faltering I pray:
  'Lord, I do believe,
  help me overcome my unbelief.'
Amen.

Victims of War

236

Lord of all,
  hear me now as I pray for victims of war.
I pray for those across the world
  who bear the scars of conflict –
  the injured, maimed and mentally distressed,
  those who have lost their limbs,
  their reason or their loved ones,
  their lives blighted by the horrors of war.
I pray for those left homeless or as refugees,
  those who have lost their livelihoods and security,
  and those who still live in daily fear for their lives.
I pray for children who have been orphaned,
  for parents who mourn their children,
  and for husbands and wives
  who have lost their partners –

countless families whose lives
will never be the same again.
Lord of all,
grant that the time will come
when divisions will be overcome,
evil conquered
and hatred ended;
a day when people everywhere
will live in harmony
and enjoy lasting peace.
Inspire all to work towards that goal,
in the name of Christ.
Amen.

Leaders

237

Living God,
I pray for all whose decisions influence
the stability of this world:
for international leaders and rulers,
for politicians and diplomats,
for national governments
and the United Nations council –
those whose decisions and negotiations
affect the lives of so many
and in whose hands peace ultimately lies.
Grant them wisdom in all they do,
courage to make tough decisions when necessary
but also a desire to work
for justice and peace whenever possible.
I pray for those in the armed forces,
charged with keeping the peace
in countries across the world –
their work involving months away
from family and friends
and often danger to themselves.

Grant them courage and sensitivity,
    and protect them in all they do.
I pray for security and intelligence services
    in this world of so much uncertainty –
    those who work to forestall and prevent terrorism;
    to track down those who aim to destroy human life
    randomly and indiscriminately.
Grant them insight,
    determination,
    and skill.
Sovereign God,
    guide those entrusted with the future of this planet,
    so that the causes of conflict may be overcome
    and a more secure future ensured for all.
In the name of Christ I ask it.
Amen.

238

Sovereign God,
    hear my prayer for all those
    to whom you have entrusted positions
    of leadership and responsibility.
Grant them wisdom in their decisions,
    courage to hold fast to what is right,
    integrity in their dealings
    and a genuine commitment to the good
    of all those they serve.
Guide them to know and do your will,
    for your kingdom's sake.
Amen.

For Healing and Healers

239

Lord Jesus Christ,
    I remember today how, throughout your ministry,
    you looked to bring healing and wholeness.

I remember how you touched the lepers,
>   restored sight to the blind,
>   cured the sick,
>   and helped the lame to walk;
>   how you brought hope to the broken-hearted
>   and those crushed in spirit,
>   peace of mind to those who were troubled,
>   and forgiveness to those burdened by guilt or failure.
Lord Jesus Christ,
>   I bring before you all in any kind of need,
>   praying again for your healing and renewing touch
>   in body, mind and spirit,
>   this and every day.
Restore them and make them whole,
>   by your grace.
Amen.

240

Lord Jesus Christ,
>   as you reached out to the sick and suffering
>   throughout your earthly ministry,
>   bringing wholeness and healing to so many,
>   reach out now through all who minister to body,
>   mind and spirit.
Through them grant your renewing, restoring touch.
Amen.

Kingdom of God

241

Gracious God,
   I mistakenly think sometimes of your kingdom
   in terms of the distant future –
   a time and a place yet to come –
   but you make it plain in the teaching of Jesus
   that it is already present
   and that you want each of us to commit ourselves
   to helping it grow here on earth.
Inspire me through all those who have had
   sufficient faith and dedication
   to attempt to do just that,
   catching a vision of what life can be,
   and striving to translate that vision into reality.
Help me to learn from them
   and to understand that you are at work in this world.
Teach me faithfully to offer my service
   and to work as far as I can to see your will done
   and your kingdom come in all its glory.
Amen.

242

Gracious God,
   you have promised that in the fullness of time
   your kingdom will come;
   a kingdom in which there will be
   no more war or violence,
   no more hatred or injustice,
   no more sickness, suffering or sorrow,
   but in which all will dwell in peace.
It is a vision that gives me hope and inspiration,
   and I long for the day when,
   together with all your people,
   I shall see it realised.

Yet there are times when it is hard to keep on trusting,
   a struggle to keep faith alive.
When I look at the sin and suffering in our world,
   the corruption, oppression and violence
   that seems so rife,
   I cannot help wondering if hope
   is simply a vain delusion,
   a chasing after the wind.
Teach me to go on believing,
   even when everything seems to count
   against such belief.
Help me to trust that your will shall be done,
   and, in faith, to do whatever I can,
   however small it may seem,
   to bring your kingdom nearer.
Amen.

243
Gracious God,
   I long for the day when your world
   will be as you want it to be:
   a world in which you will lift up the lowly
   and fill the hungry with good things;
   in which love and justice shall triumph,
   evil be ended
   and the meek inherit the earth.
Give me confidence that such a day will come,
   and, more than that,
   give me the resolve to help make it happen.
Help me to respond as best I can
   to the many millions who cry out for help,
   and so to play my part in bringing the dawn
   of your kingdom closer.
Amen.

244

Loving God,

    help me to see around me the seeds of your kingdom,
    and to nurture them lovingly until that day dawns
    when your will is done and you are all in all.

Amen.

Laughter

245

Loving God,
   I thank you for the things in life that make me laugh,
   the things that bring a smile to my face.
I thank you for a sense of humour
   helping me to see the funny side of life,
   enabling me to share a joke even when it is on me.
I thank you for those with the special gift
   of bringing laughter to others,
   bringing a little light relief
   into the seriousness of our world.
I know that there is a time to weep and a time to laugh,
   a place for solemnity and a place for humour –
   help me to get the balance right in my life.
Teach me to appreciate your gift of laughter,
   and to share it with those around me.
Amen.

246

   Lord of all, teach me never to laugh *at* others,
   but, when appropriate, to laugh *with* them,
   joyfully celebrating your gift of life in all its richness.
Amen.

247

Gracious Lord,
   send me out with laughter in my eyes,
   a smile on my lips,
   a song in my heart
   and merriment in my soul,
   and so may I share the joy that you have given me,
   to the glory of your name.
Amen.

248

Sovereign God,
    teach me that there is a time to grieve
    and a time to laugh,
    a time to be serious and a time to celebrate,
    a time for solemnity and a time for fun.
Help me to know the difference.
Amen.

Loving God

249

Gracious God,
    so dwell within me that I will rejoice
    each day at all your mercies
    and love you with heart and soul and mind.
Amen.

250

Gracious God,
    take my love for you
    and fan it into a mighty flame
    so that I may love you as you deserve,
    to the glory of your name.
Amen.

251

Sovereign God,
    teach me what it means
    to love you with body,
    mind and soul,
    and help me to be as committed to you
    as you are to me,
    through Jesus Christ my Lord.
Amen.

Loving others

252

Lord Jesus Christ,
  forgive me that so often I love only myself,
  my every thought for my own welfare,
  my own ends,
  my own esteem,
  my own pleasures.
Forgive me that, at best,
  I reserve my love for the exclusive few –
  family, friends and relations.
Teach me to reach out to this troubled, divided world,
  recognising the call of my neighbour
  in the cry of the needy.
Teach me what it means to belong
  not just to the community of faith
  but also to the family of humankind,
  and in serving them may I equally serve you,
  to the glory of your name.
Amen.

253

Lord,
  I am told that the strongest survive –
  that in this world it's a question of never mind the rest
  so long as I'm all right.
Yet you call me to another way –
  to the way of humility, sacrifice and self-denial.
You stand accepted wisdom on its head,
  claiming that the meek shall inherit the earth
  and that those who are willing to lose their life
  will truly find it.
Lord,
  it is hard to believe in this way of yours,

and harder still to live by it,
for it runs contrary to everything
I know about human nature,
yet I have seen for myself that the world's way
leads so often to hurt, sorrow and division.
Give me, then, courage to live out
the foolishness of the gospel,
and to bring closer the kingdom of Christ
here on earth.
In his name I ask it.
Amen.

254

Lord Jesus Christ,
you summed up the law in one simple word: 'love'.
Forgive me that though I often talk about love
I rarely show it in practice.
Forgive me everything in my life
that has denied that love:
the angry words and unkind comments,
the thoughtless deeds and careless actions,
the sorrow I have brought rather than joy,
the hurt rather than healing,
the care I have failed to express,
support I have refused to offer,
and forgiveness I have been unwilling to extend.
Help me to look to you who showed love in action –
a love that bears all things,
believes all things,
hopes all things,
endures all things –
and help me truly to realise that unless I have that,
then all my words, faith and religion
count for nothing.
Amen.

255
Gracious God,
  give me courage, faith and humility
  to let go of hatred
  and to follow the way of love.
Amen.

256
Gracious God,
  take the little love I have,
  nurture, deepen, and expand it,
  until I have learned what love really means,
  until your love flows through my heart,
  until love is all in all.
Amen.

257
Gracious God,
  teach me the secret of a love that goes on loving,
  despite all it faces.
Amen.

258
Lord Jesus Christ,
  you tell me that the whole law
  is summed up in the command to love:
  help me to understand what that means,
  so that it may shape my decisions,
  my attitudes and my life, to your glory.
Amen.

259
Gracious God,
  teach me to forgive as you have forgiven me,
  to care as you care for me,
  and to love as you love all.
Amen.

Peace

260

God of peace,
   quieten my heart
   and help me to be still in your presence.
I find this so hard,
   for my life is full of noise and confusion,
   a host of demands and responsibilities
   seeming to press in upon me from every side,
   consuming my time and sapping my energy.
I run here and there,
   doing this and that,
   always something else to think about,
   another pressing matter demanding my attention –
   and then suddenly,
   in the middle of it all,
   I stop and realise I have forgotten you,
   the one I depend on to give me strength
   and to calm my spirit.
God of peace,
   I offer you now this little space I have made
   in the frantic scramble of life.
Meet with me,
   so that I may return to my daily routine
   with a new perspective,
   an inner tranquillity,
   and a sense of quiet trust.
So may I use *all* my time more effectively
   in the service of your kingdom,
   through Jesus Christ my Lord.
Amen.

261

Gracious God,
    you have promised to all who love you
    a peace that passes understanding.
Forgive me that I have failed to make this my own.
I rush about, my mind preoccupied with problems.
I brood over situations I cannot hope to change,
    magnifying them out of all proportion.
I worry about what the future may hold
    instead of focusing on the present moment
    and living each day as it comes.
Teach me that you hold all things in your hands
    and that, even when my worries prove justified,
    you will give me strength to get through.
Whatever clouds may appear on the horizon
    and whatever storms life might throw against me,
    may my mind be at rest,
    my spirit at peace
    and my heart at ease,
    through Jesus Christ my Lord.
Amen.

262

Lord Jesus Christ,
    teach me not just to be *at* peace
    but also to work *for* peace,
    to the glory of your name.
Amen.

263

Lord Jesus Christ,
    speak your word
    and calm the troubled waters of my life,
    the turmoil of mind and restlessness of spirit,
    granting the peace that you alone can give.
Amen.

Praise

264

Mighty God,
  enthroned in splendour,
  crowned with glory,
  ruler over all,
  I owe my life to you.
Eternal God,
  moving throughout history,
  giving your word,
  calling your people,
  I owe my hope to you.
Living God,
  full of love,
  full of kindness,
  full of compassion,
  I owe my joy to you.
Gentle God,
  speaking through your Spirit,
  through the quietness,
  through your still, small voice,
  I owe my peace to you.
Gracious God,
  abounding in love,
  slow to anger,
  rich in mercy,
  I owe my all to you.
Lord of all,
  my strength and shield,
  my rock and my fortress,
  my God and my Redeemer,
  I owe my worship to you.
Receive my praise.
Amen.

265

Sovereign God,

    I can hardly begin to comprehend your power,

    barely grasp the extent of your love

    and scarcely start to fathom

    the awesome breadth of your purpose.

I glimpse only a little of the truth,

    yet that little causes me

    to gasp in wonder and kneel in homage.

Receive my praise,

    for I offer it in humble and reverent worship.

Amen.

266

Sovereign God,

    your greatness fills the heavens,

    your power sustains the universe,

    your love supports all creation

    and your purpose extends to the ends of the earth,

    yet you have time for the very least of us –

    time even for me!

For that most awesome of truths,

    I give you my praise.

Amen.

267

Almighty God,

    yours is the hand that created the universe,

    the power that shapes the course of history,

    the love that moves through all things

    and the grace that opens up the way to life.

Receive my praise,

    and open my heart to know you better each day,

    until that great day when I meet you face to face

    and rejoice in the wonder of your presence.

Amen.

268
Mighty God,
   though I stretch my imagination to the limit,
   I barely begin to glimpse how wonderful you are.
Though you sometimes seem distant, you are ever near.
Whatever I face, wherever I am,
   you are there, seen or unseen,
   your hand always at work.
For the constancy of your love
   and the faithfulness of your purpose,
   I give you my praise,
   in the name of Christ.
Amen.

269
Living God,
   for your greatness beyond imagining,
   your grace beyond deserving,
   your goodness beyond measuring
   and your love beyond comparing,
   I give you my praise in awe and wonder.
Amen.

270
Living God,
   you have given me joy that knows no bounds,
   mercy beyond all my deserving,
   hope that can never be exhausted,
   peace that passes understanding
   and love that exceeds anything
   I can ever ask or think of.
To you be glory, praise and honour,
   now and always.
Amen.

Prayer

271

Gracious God,

I thank you that I can open my heart to you in prayer,
that I can pour out my innermost needs
and share my deepest thoughts
in the knowledge that you are there,
always ready to listen and understand.

So once more I lay my life before you,

open to your gaze:
the bad as well as the good,
the doubt as well as the faith,
the sorrow as well as the joy,
the despair as well as the hope.

I bring my feelings of anger as well as peace,

of hatred as well as love,
of confusion as well as certainty,
of fear as well as trust.

I bring them honestly to you,

so that I may discover the renewing love
that only you can offer –
a love that frees me to live as you would have me live,
and that allows me to be the person
you would have me be!

Hear now my prayer,

in the name of Christ.

Amen.

Asking in Faith

272

Gracious God,

I don't have to tell you that my prayer life is weak,
and my faith poor,
for you know it already, all too well.

I hesitate to pray,
   in case you do not grant my requests.
I hesitate to ask,
   in case I am seeking the wrong things.
Teach me that you are a God
   who listens and delights to respond.
Save me from a lack of trust
   that frustrates your purpose,
   and closes my mind to your love.
Give me ears to hear,
   eyes to see,
   and a heart that truly believes,
   through Jesus Christ my Lord.
Amen.

273
Loving God,
   you long to shower me with blessings,
   to fill my life with good things,
   yet there are times when,
   through my weakness of faith,
   I frustrate your gracious purpose
   and deprive myself of the inexpressible riches
   you so freely offer.
I do not seek,
   so I do not find.
I do not ask,
   so I do not receive.
I concern myself with the fleeting pleasures
   of the moment
   and so fail to grasp treasures that endure for eternity.
Forgive me the shallowness of my values
   and the limitations of my understanding.
Teach me to set my heart on those things
   that can truly satisfy,
   and that you so yearn to share with me.
In the name of Christ I ask it.
Amen.

Essentials of Prayer

274

Living God,
   forgive my superficial understanding of prayer –
   the way I abuse and distort it,
   using it as a lever to coerce you
   rather than seeing it as a personal encounter
   through which I might grow closer to you each day.
Teach me to seek what you will,
   rather than what I desire;
   to be open to your guidance,
   however much it may conflict with my own wishes.
Teach me to obey your voice.
Amen.

275

Living God,
   you invite me to talk *with* you in prayer
   but instead I talk *at* you.
You invite me to seek your will
   but I attempt rather to impose my own.
You tell me that you know all my needs,
   yet I present you with a list of demands
   and requests.
Forgive me the way I misunderstand
   and abuse this most precious gift.
Teach me not only to speak but also to listen,
   not just to seek but also to find,
   not simply to bring my requests
   but also to respond to your call.
Remind me that there is a time for words
   and a time to keep silent,
   and help me to make room for both.
Amen.

276

Loving God,
 I am good at talking about prayer
 but poor when it comes to praying.
I find that the words just don't come
 or that I end up repeating the same old things.
I speak of a conversation,
 but the reality is more typically a monologue,
 and on the rare occasions that I make time to listen,
 I struggle to hear your voice.
As a result I all too often give up,
 prayer pushed to one side,
 conveniently forgotten,
 until some tragedy or crisis awakens me
 to my need of you.
Forgive me for abusing prayer,
 using it as an excuse to avoid real service.
Forgive me my misguided prayers,
 concerned only with my interests rather than yours.
Forgive me my neglect of prayer,
 my reluctance to take it seriously
 or to devote time to you.
Teach me what it means to wrestle in prayer
 and so may I use it as you intended,
 to the glory of your name.
Amen.

277

Living God,
 there are times when I pray
 but the words just won't come,
 and times when I simply don't know what to pray for.
There are times when I forget to pray,
 or when my prayers are casual and half-hearted,
 squeezed in as an afterthought at the end of the day.

Thank you, then, that I am not alone in prayer,
    that your response does not depend
    solely on my efforts.
Thank you for the work of the Spirit within,
    articulating my deepest thoughts and needs,
    and for the faithfulness of Christ,
    constantly interceding on my behalf.
Living God,
    hear *my* words now
    and *their* prayer always,
    and, in your mercy, reach out in love.
Amen.

278

Loving Lord,
    you are always looking to respond to my needs,
    constantly reaching out to touch my life
    with your love,
    yet all too often I fail to seek the help
    you long to give me.
I trust in my own strength;
    I try this, that and everything else;
    and I only remember you
    when I reach the end of my tether
    and there is no one left to turn to.
Forgive me for relegating you to the periphery
    rather than putting you at the centre of my life.
Forgive me for treating you as a last resort
    instead of a first recourse.
Teach me to bring my needs to you,
    knowing that, though you may not always
    respond as I want you to,
    you will always respond in love,
    providing for my needs,
    granting me peace

and bringing the wholeness
   that you alone can give.
In your name I ask it.
Amen.

Unanswered Prayer

279
Living God,
   there are times in my life,
   all too many,
   when my prayers don't seem to be answered.
There are times when, for all my striving,
   I do not hear your voice or understand your will.
Yet you *do* respond,
   if only I have ears to hear and eyes to see –
   through the people around me,
   through the events of life,
   through the voice of conscience.
In innumerable ways you prompt me,
   not dictating my every step,
   not mapping out the future,
   but inviting me to share in the work of your kingdom
   and the fulfilment of your purpose.
Living God,
   help me to listen –
   help me to hear.
Amen.

280
Lord Jesus Christ,
   it is hard to keep faith
   when you do not seem to answer my prayers;
   harder still when you seem remote and disinterested,
   seemingly unmoved by my pleas.

Teach me that sometimes
   you are speaking precisely
   through that apparent lack of response,
   challenging me to look more deeply into my situation
   and to broaden my horizons.
Yet teach me also that you *do* hear
   and delight to respond,
   and so may I never be discouraged from asking,
   in your name.
Amen.

281
Living God,
   I bring to you those times when I call to you for help
   and you seem silent;
   those days when I do not hear your voice
   no matter how I listen for it.
Help me to understand that even when I feel alone,
   you are listening,
   and even when you seem far away,
   you are always near.
Give me faith to hold on,
   courage to trust in your promises,
   and humility to recognise that your answer will come
   in your own time and your own way.
May that knowledge sustain and inspire me,
   whatever I may face,
   through Jesus Christ my Lord.
Amen.

282
Living God,
   when you do not seem to answer,
   help me to listen harder,
   and when you *do* speak,
   teach me to listen and respond;
   through Jesus Christ my Lord.
Amen.

Questions of faith

283
Eternal God,
    there are times when I find life a puzzle,
    your purpose a mystery,
    experience seeming to contradict everything
    I believe about you.
I try to make sense of it all,
    but without success,
    satisfactory answers always seeming to elude me.
Teach me at such moments to trust in you,
    recognising that what the world counts as folly
    is often true wisdom.
Help me to live with riddles and apparent paradox,
    and to keep on searching for truth,
    confident that in the fullness of time
    you will make all things clear.
I ask it in the name of Christ.
Amen.

284
Gracious God,
    I thank you for all you have revealed to me in Christ
    and for the faith you have put into my heart,
    but I thank you also that there is more to understand
    in my continuing journey of discovery.
So I bring you the things I don't understand,
    the statements of faith that don't seem to make sense
    and the events of life that seem to contradict
    what I have been taught of you.
I bring you my certainty and my uncertainty,
    those areas where faith is sure
    and those where it teeters on the edge of collapse.

Give me sufficient trust
   to acknowledge my questions openly
   and to offer them honestly to you in prayer.
Save me from taking refuge in ritual or dogma,
   but teach me rather to face
   the challenges that life brings
   and to work through my faith in the light of them,
   so that, having been tested, it may grow the stronger,
   able to face all and still to stand,
   through Jesus Christ my Lord.
Amen.

285
Living God,
   day by day I have to choose:
   to make decisions about right and wrong,
   good and evil.
Sometimes the choice is clear, sometimes confusing,
   sometimes easy, sometimes hard,
   sometimes mattering little, sometimes much,
   but, whatever the case, I need to seek your will
   and to make up my mind as to the best way forward.
Help me to decide wisely,
   for there is so much I do not understand,
   so many complicated and confusing areas of life.
Grant me faith to wrestle with such matters,
   confident that you can use them
   to lead me to new insights
   and a deeper awareness of your sovereign purpose,
   to the glory of your name.
Amen.

286
Living God,
   there is so much suffering in this world of ours,
   so much pain, sorrow and evil.

It is hard sometimes to reconcile all this
    with it being your world too,
    created by you and precious in your sight.
I search desperately for answers,
    clinging first to this and then to that,
    and underneath there are times
    when my faith begins to crumble.
Teach me that, though I cannot always see it,
    you are there,
    sharing in my anguish,
    carrying in yourself the agony of creation
    as it groans under the weight of imperfection.
Teach me that you will not rest
    until that day when all suffering is ended,
    evil is no more
    and your kingdom is established,
    and in that assurance give me strength
    to face each day,
    whatever it might bring.
Amen.

287
Lord,
    you know my faith isn't perfect.
There is much that I don't understand,
    much that I question,
    and much that is not all it ought to be.
Despite my love for you,
    I find it difficult to trust as I know I should,
    the things I don't believe
    triumphing over the things I do.
Yet, for all its weakness,
    you know that my faith is real,
    and you know that I long to serve you better.
Take, then, what I am and what I offer,
    and, through your grace, provide what I lack,
    until the faith I profess with my lips

   may be echoed in my life,
   and made complete.
Amen.

288

Loving God,
   sometimes I cannot help but ask 'Why?'
'Why me?'
'Why this?'
'Why anything?'
There is so much I do not understand,
   so much that apparently contradicts my faith,
   leaving me groping for answers,
   and all too easily I feel guilty
   about having such questions,
   afraid that somehow I am letting the side down
   through doing so.
Yet in my heart I know there is no point pretending,
   for I can never deceive you.
So help me honestly to admit that
   there are things I cannot make sense of,
   and to trust that though *I* may never understand,
   you do.
Amen.

289

Loving God,
   I *do* believe.
I believe that in Jesus
   you have shown the way, the truth and the life.
Yet alongside faith there is also doubt.
I do not have all the answers,
   and sometimes I seem only to have questions.
Yet I believe that those questions, honestly asked,
   can lead me to a deeper understanding
   of who you are
   and what you have done.

So today I offer you not just my faith
   but also my doubt,
   praying that you will use both
   to lead me closer to you.
Amen.

290
Sovereign God,
   I cannot help wondering sometimes
   about the justice of life.
I see so much that is wrong,
   so much that I cannot make sense of,
   and I ask myself why you stand by and let it happen.
Day after day, I watch helplessly
   as truth is trodden underfoot,
   love exploited,
   and the innocent suffer,
   while those who least deserve it seem to flourish.
Help me, confronted by such enigmas,
   not to lose heart.
Teach me to recognise that loving you
   brings its own rewards,
   greater than any this world can offer,
   and remind me also that the time will come
   when everyone will answer to you,
   and justice will prevail.
Amen.

291
Lord,
   so often I don't understand what is happening to me.
I am swept along by a tide of circumstances
   and I look in vain to find any pattern
   that might give meaning to it all.
My fleeting span is a confusing riddle
   from which you can seem painfully absent.

Yet you are there, even though I cannot see you,
   patiently weaving the broken strands of life
   into an intricate tapestry.
Teach me, then, to trust in you and to live by faith
   until that day when the picture is complete
   and I understand at last
   all the ways you have been working
   to bring order out of chaos,
   good out of evil,
   joy out of sorrow,
   and life out of death.
In Christ's name I pray.
Amen.

292
Loving God,
   I do not want to be tossed around
   by every wind of change
   or swayed by every passing idea,
   but neither do I want to be so set in my ways
   that I am closed to new insights into truth
   and fresh perspectives on your word.
Forgive me those times when I have been just that,
   so convinced of my own rightness
   that I have refused to hear what others are saying –
   closing my ears to that which unsettles me
   and shying away from the possibility
   that my horizons need to be broader.
Give me true humility to listen to other opinions,
   to explore different possibilities,
   to face searching questions,
   and to adapt my views where appropriate,
   confident that truth is strong enough to be tested
   and to emerge the stronger for it.
In the name of Christ I ask it.
Amen.

293
Sovereign God,
    stronger than I can ever comprehend,
    greater than I can ever imagine,
    wiser than I can ever understand
    and more loving than I can ever dream,
    teach me to consecrate my mind to you,
    as well as my heart,
    using my intellect to wrestle with questions of faith
    and to grow in understanding.
Yet teach me also when I need to recognise
    the limitations of the human mind.
Show me when I need simply to trust,
    knowing that you are a God above all gods,
    made known through Christ my Lord.
Amen.

294
Almighty God,
    when faith is a puzzle and I look in vain for answers,
    teach me when to keep on searching
    and when I must learn to live with mystery.
Amen.

295
Sovereign God,
    save me from a faith that asks no questions,
    and from a faith that asks too many,
    through Jesus Christ, my Lord.
Amen.

296
Gracious God,
    give me courage to ask questions,
    faith to live with them,
    and grace to grow through them,
    to the glory of your name.
Amen.

297

Mighty and mysterious God,
　　when I cannot make sense of the jigsaw of my life,
　　remind me that now I see only in part,
　　but one day I will see you face to face
　　and know you even as I am fully known.
Amen.

298

Lord of all,
　　give me sufficient trust to acknowledge
　　my questions openly and to offer them
　　honestly to you in prayer,
　　confident that they are a part of faith,
　　able to lead me to new insights
　　and a deeper understanding of your purpose,
　　through Jesus Christ my Lord.
Amen.

Quiet reflection

299

Lord Jesus Christ,
    time and again throughout your ministry
    you made time to be still,
    to draw away from the crowds
    so that in the quietness
    you could reflect on your calling.
You needed those moments,
    just as I need them in my turn.
So now I have made a space in my life,
    away from the daily demands,
    away from the usual routine.
I am here, Lord, with time for you,
    in stillness and in quietness to seek your will.
Use these moments
    to refresh me,
    to feed me,
    to challenge and inspire me.
Fill them with your love
    and so may I be filled to overflowing,
    by your grace.
Amen.

300

Sovereign God,
    I am here to worship you,
    having made a space in my life to pause and reflect.
I come to listen to your word,
    and to ponder in the silence
    what you would say to me.
I come to hear your voice,
    and in the stillness to receive your guidance.

Open my eyes to your presence,
   my heart to your love
   and my mind to your will.
Direct my thoughts,
   enlarge my understanding,
   and shape my life,
   so that I may live and work for you,
   to the glory of your name.
Amen.

301

Living God,
   in the rush and bustle of each day
   I all too often lose sight of you,
   my mind occupied by the responsibilities,
   demands and difficulties confronting me.
Instead of turning to you,
   I am sucked in ever deeper,
   getting things out of all perspective
   and denying myself the strength I need to meet them.
Teach me to find time for you,
   if only for a few moments,
   so that I may hear your voice and discern your will.
Teach me to step back and take stock,
   so that I may then step forward,
   renewed in faith,
   strengthened in spirit,
   and equipped for whatever you may ask.
In Jesus' name I ask it.
Amen.

302

Living God,
   too often I rush from one thing to the next,
   preoccupied with the demands

and responsibilities of each day,
and wondering where I might find the strength
to see me through.
Yet instead of turning to you
I struggle on as best I can.
Teach me to create space in my life for you,
to make a few moments every day
in which I can be quiet and still,
and teach me to do that not as an afterthought
but instinctively,
recognising that when I give you your proper place,
everything else will fit into place as well.
In Christ's name I ask it.
Amen.

303
Loving God,
in all the stress and rush of life
it is so easy to forget you
and to lose my way.
In the press of each day,
preoccupied with my problems, pursuits,
plans and responsibilities
I allow you to be crowded out.
I strive and fret over things that cannot satisfy,
I brood over what is unimportant,
frantically suppressing
that sense of emptiness deep within.
Teach me to untangle myself
from everything that enslaves me
and to open my heart afresh to you,
so that I might find rest and nourishment
for my soul
and life in all its fullness,
through Jesus Christ my Lord.
Amen.

304

Loving God,
   I live at such a hectic pace,
   my life so busy and pressurised,
   with never a moment to spare.
Yet so often I forget the one thing I really need:
   time to pause and ponder,
   to take stock of my life and reflect on your goodness
   so that I might understand
   what it is that you would say to me.
Draw near to me now in these few moments of quietness.
Teach me to be still and to know your presence,
   through Jesus Christ my Lord.
Amen.

305

Gracious God,
   help me to hear again your still small voice,
   your word even in the silence,
   and to recognise that,
   though sometimes I may not see it,
   you are always there and always active,
   through Jesus Christ my Lord.
Amen.

306

Living God,
   whatever the pressures and duties of the day,
   teach me to find time for stillness,
   and, in seeing you then,
   may I see you always and everywhere,
   through the grace of Christ.
Amen.

307

Lord of all,
   I have made time and space
   to hear your voice.

Go with me now into the turmoil of life,
    with all its noise and confusion,
    all its demands and responsibilities,
    and may your peace rest with me there,
    this day and for evermore.
Amen.

308
God of the still small voice,
    teach me each day to find time
    for moments of quietness –
    time to ponder, to pray
    and to meditate on your gracious love.
Breathe peace within my soul,
    so that I may see the demands and responsibilities
    of daily life in a fresh light,
    able to meet them with rekindled faith
    and calm assurance.
Amen.

309
Sovereign God,
    open my soul to your living presence,
    so that I may glimpse your glory
    and discover the sacredness of every moment.
Amen.

310
Sovereign God,
    when I cannot discern your hand
    or sense your presence,
    help me to understand that you are no less near
    than you have ever been,
    and that, seen or unseen,
    you continue to work out your purpose.
Amen.

———— Reading the Bible ————

311

Gracious God,

    I praise you for the way your word has spoken
    to so many across the years,
    offering a lamp for their path and a faith to live by.

I thank you for the way it has spoken to me,

    stirring my imagination,
    kindling and nurturing faith,
    confronting and questioning,
    yet also renewing and uplifting,
    each day assuring me of your constant love
    and gracious purpose.

Teach me to study the Bible,

    to reflect on its meaning,
    and to seek enlightenment,
    so that I may hear your voice and respond.

Open my heart and mind to receive

    what you would say to me,
    and help me to respond in faith and action.

In Jesus' name I pray.

Amen.

312

Gracious God,

    you have spoken through the Law and Prophets,
    through words of wisdom, history and the psalms,
    through the testimony of Evangelists and Apostles
    and above all through the Word made flesh.

I praise you that I can turn to the Bible

    whenever I wish to
    and read it freely in my own tongue.

I can read new translations that help bring

    the age-old message to life,

and I have access to all kinds of resources
designed to deepen my understanding of what I read.
Forgive me that all too often
I leave the Bible sitting on a shelf,
unopened,
unexplored.
Help me to recognise how priceless it is
and teach me, in the clamour of each day,
to make time to read it,
reverently and thoughtfully,
eagerly and expectantly,
so that your voice may speak again,
offering light to my path
and the way to life in all its fullness.
Amen.

313

Living God,
teach me to read the Scriptures
not as a record of past events
but as a message
that goes on being realised in new ways today,
both in my life and in the lives of others,
by the grace of Christ.
Amen.

314

Lord Jesus Christ,
give me wisdom to hold on to truth
but also humility to recognise
that I do not have a monopoly on it.
Open my heart to your challenging
and illuminating word,
from wherever that might come,
for your name's sake.
Amen.

315

Sovereign God,
    guide me in the reading
    and understanding of Holy Scripture,
    until it becomes so much a part of me
    that your voice is heard through all I am and do,
    to the glory of your name.
Amen.

316

Sovereign God,
    as you have spoken through the Scriptures
    across the ages, speak also to me.
Give me wisdom in reading,
    sensitivity in interpreting,
    and resolve in applying them,
    so that I may grow closer to you
    and be better equipped to serve you,
    to the glory of your name.
Amen.

Relationships

Anger and Conflict

317

Living God,
    teach me when it is right to be angry:
    to rage against the things in life
    that demean and destroy,
    that feed injustice and further exploitation,
    that cheat, corrupt, wound and hurt,
    that lead the innocent astray
    and divide people from one another and from you.
Yet teach me also when anger is foolish and petty,
    more about my hurt pride than right and wrong,
    about myself than the cause I attribute anger to.
Save me, then, from the errors it might give rise to –
    thoughtless words,
    careless deeds,
    and destructive attitudes –
    and help me to control such anger
    before it controls me.
Amen.

318

Lord,
    I am not good at showing anger;
    at least, not as it is meant to be shown.
I am ready enough to show my temper,
    easily riled by the most innocuous of things,
    and capable, at my worst, of destructive fits of rage,
    but such anger is rarely justified,
    almost always serving merely
    to give vent to my feelings
    at the cost of someone else's.

Your anger is so very different,
   being not about yourself but others.
You see injustice and exploitation,
   and your blood boils for the oppressed.
You see the peddling of drugs and pornography,
   and your heart burns within you
   at the innocent led astray.
You see hatred, violence and cruelty,
   and your spirit seethes for those caught up in its wake.
Whatever destroys hope,
   denies love
   or despoils life
   arouses wrath within you.
Teach me to share that anger
   and to channel it in your service,
   committing myself to do all in my power
   to fight against evil,
   and to work for the growth of your kingdom,
   through Jesus Christ my Lord.
Amen.

319
Lord,
   it's easy to start a quarrel,
   so much harder to end it.
It's easy to see faults in others,
   far more difficult to see my own.
It's easy to destroy relationships,
   almost impossible to build them again
   once they have been broken.
Forgive me the weaknesses
   that so often create divisions,
   that separate me not simply
   from my fellow human beings
   but sometimes even from my own family and friends.

Help me –
    so far as it lies with me –
    to live in harmony with all,
    and when that harmony is broken
    teach me to act as a peacemaker,
    healing hurts,
    restoring trust and breaking down barriers.
Amen.

320

Lord Jesus Christ,
    give me grace to see the point of view of others,
    humility to accept when I am wrong
    and sensitivity in my attitude when I am right,
    so that I may live in peace with my neighbour,
    for your name's sake.
Amen.

Encouragement and Respect

321

Gracious God,
    you call us to support one another,
    to offer comfort in times of need,
    reassurance in times of fear,
    inspiration in times of challenge,
    and confidence in times of doubt.
Forgive me for so easily doing the opposite –
    finding fault,
    running down,
    criticising and condemning.
Forgive me for seeing the worst instead of the best,
    for believing the bad instead of the good,
    for so often pulling down and so rarely building up.
Teach me to recognise people's gifts and nurture them,
    to understand their problems and share them,
    to acknowledge their successes and applaud them,
    to appreciate their efforts and affirm them.

Teach me, through the faith I show in people,
 to help them attempt great things
 and expect great things;
 to look at life seeing not the obstacles
 but the opportunities,
 not the things they can't do but the things they can.
So may I help them in Christ to discover their gifts,
 recognise their true worth and fulfil their potential.
Amen.

322
Living God,
 sometimes I feel weighed down
 by the stresses and strains of daily life –
 oppressed by worry,
 unable to throw off my anxieties,
 held captive by a multitude of secret fears.
I thank you for all those
 who help me through such moments,
 who offer a shoulder to lean on,
 an arm to steady me
 and a hand to share the load.
Teach me in turn to bear the burdens of others,
 doing all I can through listening,
 understanding,
 caring and sharing,
 to offer them my help.
As you have reached out to me,
 so teach me to reach out to others,
 expressing your love and showing your care,
 to the glory of your name.
Amen.

323
Lord,
 I am so wrapped up in myself
 that I forget sometimes all I owe to others:

the support, love, encouragement and inspiration
I receive from so many.
I am swift to complain when things are not done
but slow to express gratitude when they are,
good at criticising
but poor in showing appreciation.
Help me to recognise everything others do for me
and to make a point of acknowledging it.
Help me to play my part in turn,
contributing to their lives
with equal commitment and dedication.
In Christ's name I pray.
Amen.

324

Living God,
when I am confronted by ideas I do not understand
my natural tendency is to lash out against them.
I resort to the language of insult.
I condemn rather than try to understand,
ridicule rather than reflect,
and, because of that,
so often I fail to recognise you are speaking to me,
challenging my preconceptions
and leading me on to new experiences of your love.
Living God,
when I meet people who think differently to me,
give me grace to recognise that it may be me
rather than them who needs to change.
Amen.

325

Lord Jesus Christ,
you did not come to judge or condemn the world,
but to save it.
Where others saw the bad in people,
you saw the good.

You recognised the value in everyone,
    and instilled in all a sense of worth.
Such was your willingness to welcome the unacceptable
    that many were scandalised by your behaviour.
Forgive me that I can be equally self-righteous,
    more concerned with judgement than mercy.
Forgive me for failing to see in myself the evil
    that I am so ready to see in others.
Teach me to look at the world with your eyes,
    and to deal graciously in all my relationships,
    just as you have dealt graciously with me.
Amen.

326

Gracious God,
    I know that you value everyone,
    not for what they might become
    but for what they are.
Forgive me that, all too often, I forget that truth,
    full of my own importance,
    preoccupied with self,
    harbouring vain illusions about who I am
    and what I can achieve.
I have not valued others as they deserve,
    allowing prejudices and preconceptions
    to colour my judgement
    and poison my attitudes.
I have looked down on those around me,
    failing to see the good in them,
    closed to the contribution they can make to my life.
For all those times
    when I have valued myself too much
    and others too little,
    forgive me,
    in the name of Christ.
Amen.

327

Sovereign God,
   I have been guilty of the sin of pride,
   thinking of myself more highly than I should,
   boasting of my own achievements
   and looking down on those around me.
I have not listened to your voice
   or the voice of others,
   believing instead that I know best,
   and I have been guilty of pride in more subtle ways,
   hiding my frailties behind a mask of self-sufficiency,
   denying my weaknesses
   and refusing support when it has been offered.
Forgive me, and grant me true humility:
   a willingness to listen to your voice,
   to recognise my weaknesses
   and to acknowledge my need of others,
   through Jesus Christ my Lord.
Amen.

328

Sovereign God,
   time and again you have overturned
   human expectations,
   using the most unlikely of people
   in yet more unlikely surroundings.
You have shown beyond doubt that no situation
   or person is outside the scope of your purpose –
   that you can use each one of them.
Teach me, then,
   to be open to everything you would do
   through those around me,
   and to recognise also all you can do through me,
   working in ways I would never dare to contemplate
   and can scarcely imagine.

Sovereign God,
    you recognise the potential of everyone
    and everything:
    help me to do the same.
Amen.

329

Living God,
    it is hard sometimes to say no.
I do not want to let people down.
I like to appear on top of things,
    capable of meeting every challenge,
    and I am reluctant to admit my limitations.
I am afraid of being thought selfish
    or unwilling to put myself out.
For a whole variety of reasons,
    I find it easier to say yes
    even when I know I should decline.
Teach me that there are times when I owe it to myself,
    my family or my friends to say no,
    and times also when saying yes
    will mean a job is not done properly, if at all.
Help me to do what I can,
    both in your service and in the service of others,
    but to recognise also what I can't do,
    and then grant me the courage I need to say no.
In Christ's name I pray.
Amen.

330

Living God,
    you have given me so much;
    forgive me that I still want more.
I have so many blessings to rejoice in;
    forgive me that instead
    I dwell on the pleasures I do not have.

Above all,
    forgive me for the way I allow envy
    to poison my attitude
    and colour my judgement,
    insinuating itself into the way I think, feel,
    speak and act towards others.
Teach me to appreciate everything
    that is good in my life,
    and to rejoice equally with others
    in the things that are good in theirs,
    and, most of all, teach me to celebrate
    the love you give freely to all,
    beyond measure,
    without reserve,
    now and for all eternity,
    through the grace of Christ.
Amen.

331

Loving God,
    teach me not just to thank *you*
    but to thank all who in any way enrich my life.
Help me, through word and deed,
    to show my appreciation of everything they do
    and everything they mean.
Amen.

332

Creator God,
    teach me that you did not just make some,
    but all, people in your likeness,
    and so teach me to value and respect
    everyone in the family of humankind.
Amen.

333

Lord Jesus Christ,
   as you have seen the good in me,
   so help me to see the good in others,
   for your name's sake.
Amen.

Judging

334

Almighty God,
   I have set myself up in your place so often,
   presuming I have a right to judge others.
I know it is wrong,
   and I try to stop myself,
   yet I repeatedly fall into the same trap,
   pointing the accusing finger in condemnation.
I jump to conclusions
   that say more about myself than anyone;
   I see faults in others
   yet I am blind to my own innumerable failings.
Forgive me,
   and help me to change.
Teach me to see the best rather than the worst,
   to look for good rather than evil,
   to build up rather than destroy.
Teach me to forgive as you have forgiven me,
   and to leave final judgement where it belongs:
   with you.
Amen.

335

Gracious God,
   I know how foolish it is to judge by the outside,
   yet time and again I catch myself doing it.
My mind says one thing,
   but my heart tells me another.

Even when I think I am looking deeper,
    my conditioning makes me look
    at the world in a set way,
    deceived by superficial impressions,
    failing to see the good in some and the evil in others.
Help me to see with your eyes,
    to look beyond the obvious
    to the deeper realities of life,
    and to recognise the true worth of all those around me.
Amen.

336
Living God,
    forgive me for imagining sometimes
    that I know all there is to know about people;
    for presuming to judge their abilities and qualities
    on the basis of what I understand about them.
Forgive me for questioning
    what you can do through them
    because I fail to see their true potential.
Teach me that you are able to use anyone and everyone
    in ways I have not even begun to consider.
Open my eyes, then,
    to what you are doing in those around me,
    and help me to recognise
    what you may be saying to me through them.
In Christ's name I ask it.
Amen.

337
Lord Jesus Christ,
    I thank you that you love me and accept me
    not for what I can be but for what I am.
I thank you that although you see my many weaknesses,
    still you have time for me,
    seeing the best rather than the worst.

Lord Jesus Christ,
    forgive me that all too often I see only the surface,
    judging people according to instant impressions,
    and condemning those who do not fit in
    with my view of the world.
Help me to have time for others as you have time for me.
Amen.

338
Loving God,
    you tell us not to judge others,
    but I find it so hard not to.
You tell us that on those occasions
    when we do need to judge,
    we should do so wisely,
    but again I find that so difficult,
    for although I strive to be open-minded
    and objective in the decisions I make,
    I all too rarely succeed.
I am shaped by a multitude of influences
    that make me the person I am,
    and the way I look at the world
    is determined by each one,
    so that I find it almost impossible
    to see beyond my preconceived ideas.
Even when the truth is staring me in the face
    I can fail to spot it,
    so ingrained have these ideas become.
Break through the barriers that shut my mind fast,
    and help me to see things both as they really are
    and as you can help them become.
Loving God,
    fill me with the mind of Christ,
    to his glory.
Amen.

339
Sovereign God,
 like the Pharisees of old
 I am often guilty of finding fault with others
 when in reality the problem lies in myself.
I am so busy looking for things to criticise
 that I fail to recognise my own many weaknesses.
Day by day, I am guilty of hypocrisy
 without even beginning to realise it.
Forgive me for the way I preach one rule for others
 while reserving another quite different
 rule for myself.
Forgive me for dwelling on the letter of the law
 whilst completely overlooking the spirit.
Teach us to recognise that your will is summed up
 in one simple commandment:
 to love;
 and so work within me
 that your love may characterise
 my every thought and action.
In the name of Christ I ask it.
Amen.

340
Lord of all,
 deliver me from a faith so rigid that
 it is closed to new insights,
 from a vision so narrow that
 it is closed to new horizons,
 from dogmas so rigid that
 I am closed to your Spirit,
 and from convictions so fixed that
 I am closed to other Christians.
Open my eyes to you and to others,
 in Jesus' name.
Amen.

341

Sovereign God,
    save me from being so full of myself
    and preoccupied with my rightness
    that I have no time to learn from others.
Deliver me from being so limited by my own horizons
    and parochial concerns that I have no time for you.
Teach me that,
    if I would grow in faith,
    service and witness,
    I must first grow closer to you and all your people.
Amen.

Sensitivity

342

Lord,
    I thank you for the wonderful gift of words:
    the ability through language
    to communicate with others,
    to express thoughts and feelings,
    to share information,
    to move, challenge and inspire,
    to offer ideas,
    to bring comfort.
Forgive me for the way I turn something so special
    into something so ugly,
    capable of causing such devastation.
Teach me to think more carefully about what I say
    and to speak always with the intention of helping
    rather than hurting.
Help me to use words wisely,
    in the name of Jesus Christ,
    the Word made flesh.
Amen.

343
Living God,
    teach me what it means to be true to myself,
    faithful to you, yet sensitive to others,
    through Jesus Christ my Lord.
Amen.

Service

344
Lord,
    I need your love,
    your mercy,
    your guidance
    and your peace,
    for without you my soul is restless,
    my life impoverished
    and my destiny hopeless.
But I thank you too
    that, incredibly, you are a God who has need of me,
    a God who has chosen to make yourself
    dependent on human cooperation.
You need my faith and trust;
    my hands and feet;
    my willingness to speak in service and witness;
    my commitment to you in body, mind and soul.
Living God,
    I marvel that you need me as much as I need you,
    but I thank you for that great truth,
    that awesome privilege
    and that amazing responsibility.
Help me to honour the trust you have placed in me,
    through honouring Jesus Christ my Lord.
In his name I pray.
Amen.

345

Lord Jesus Christ,
   I want to serve you,
   and I like to believe I do,
   but unwittingly I can turn even my faith
   into a way of serving self.
I gain strength through fellowship and worship,
   but neglect your call to mission.
I focus on my own concerns in prayer
   and forget about the world beyond.
Even my deeds of kindness can finally
   be more about my own sense of righteousness
   than the needs of those I think I am serving.
Lord Jesus,
   overcome the stranglehold of self
   and help me to understand
   that true discipleship brings its own reward,
   for the more I give the more I shall receive.
In your mercy,
   hear my prayer.
Amen.

346

Lord Jesus Christ,
   I have been guilty of focusing on individual blessing
   at the cost of corporate responsibility,
   more concerned with what I will receive from you
   than with what I should give to others.
Forgive me for turning the gospel on its head,
   tailoring it to suit my own ends
   rather than allowing it to renew my life.
Forgive me for being so preoccupied with heaven
   that I forget needs here on earth.
Teach me that, though I can never earn my salvation,
   I need to show the reality of my faith
   through the way I live.

Show me where you would have me serve,
    and help me to love you as you love all.
Amen.

347
Lord Jesus Christ,
    help me to show my faith
    not just in abstract love for the world
    but also in practical service to those around me.
In my daily relationships –
    at home,
    at work,
    at leisure,
    at church;
    whenever and wherever it might be –
    teach me to live out my faith in such a way
    that my life embodies the claims
    and truth of the gospel,
    to the glory of your name.
Amen.

348
Lord Jesus Christ,
    teach me to serve you,
    not for any recognition I might receive,
    but for the joy of contributing to your kingdom.
Amen.

349
Lord Jesus Christ,
    as you are always thinking of me,
    reaching out in love,
    so teach me to reach out to others,
    for your name's sake.
Amen.

350

Lord Jesus Christ,
   who became poor for our sake,
   teach me, having so much,
   to remember the many who have so little,
   and, in responding to them,
   may I respond also to you.
Amen.

351

Lord Jesus Christ,
   teach me that a little in your hands
   can achieve more than a fortune in mine,
   and so inspire me to give generously in your service,
   to the glory of your name.
Amen.

Within the Church

352

Gracious God,
   I thank you for the great honour of belonging to Christ
   and being part of his Body.
Teach me what that means.
Help me to contribute to the life of your people,
   through offering my time, money, gifts and service.
Help me to make time for fellowship,
   so that I may know the strength
   that comes through sharing joys and sorrows,
   joining in prayer and worship,
   and learning through the experience of others.
Help me to appreciate the enrichment that comes
   through being an active member of your family,
   and so may I make that membership
   more real each day,
   through Jesus Christ my Lord.
Amen.

353

Lord Jesus Christ,
    there are some people I find it easy to relate to,
    others I find hard;
    some I am naturally drawn towards,
    others I shy away from;
    some I enjoy working with,
    others who constantly rub me up the wrong way.
Yet you have called me into a family
    in which all have their place,
    however different they may be.
Teach me to see such differences as strengths,
    and to be ready to learn from others.
Amen.

354

Lord Jesus Christ,
    help me to worship you
    not just for these few moments
    or in one small part of my life,
    but in all my words and deeds –
    through the person I am and the life I lead,
    the praise I bring you and the service I offer.
In your name I ask it.
Amen.

355

Lord of all,
    teach me to recognise
    that everyone has a place in your purpose
    and a contribution to make to your kingdom,
    and so help me to see beyond the barriers that keep
    us apart to everything that draws us together,
    through Jesus Christ our Lord.
Amen.

356
Sovereign God,
   teach me that,
   if you can use me,
   you can use anyone.
Amen.

357
Sovereign God,
   teach me not to think too highly of myself,
   nor too little of others.
Amen.

358
Living God,
   teach me that I need others just as they need me,
   and so may I discharge my responsibilities
   faithfully within the great company
   of your people,
   to the glory of your name.
Amen.

Strength in weakness

359
Gracious God,
   there are times in my life when I feel up against it
   and when everything seems to conspire against me.
I look at the problems confronting me,
   and I feel small and helpless,
   powerless to do anything about them.
Yet you are a God who, time and again,
   has used those who seem insignificant in this world
   to achieve great things;
   a God who has overcome the strong through the weak
   and who is able to accomplish within us
   far more than we can ask or even imagine.
Help me, then, when I am faced by obstacles
   that seem insurmountable,
   to put my trust in you,
   knowing that you will give me the strength I need,
   when I need it.
Amen.

360
Loving God,
   I haven't much to give,
   and of what I do have I give you only a fraction.
To think that you can use this
   stretches credulity to the limit,
   and yet, across the years, you have taken
   what the world regards as insignificant
   and repeatedly used it to transform situations.
Teach me, then,
   to look not at the feebleness of my resources,
   nor the awesome scale of human need,
   but to recognise instead your sovereign power,

and so, in faith,
may I offer my money,
my witness
and my service
to the glory of your name.
Amen.

361
Loving God,
  I find it hard sometimes
  to shoulder my responsibilities,
  preferring instead to share the burden with others,
  but there are times
  when I have to stand on my own two feet
  and accept the challenges life brings.
Help me, when those moments come,
  to recognise that, however helpless I might feel,
  and however weak I might think I am,
  I can rely on you to see me through.
Teach me that I am never alone,
  for you are always with me,
  giving me the help I need to meet
  whatever challenges may lie ahead.
So, trusting in your strength,
  may I faithfully discharge
  the responsibilities you give me.
Amen.

362
Loving God,
  I do not like living with weakness.
I want to feel strong,
  in control of my destiny,
  able to stand up against
  whatever life might throw at me,
  and I resent anything which threatens
  that sense of security.

Yet, across the years,
   you have repeatedly turned this world's
   expectations upside-down,
   your values totally different from my own.
You humble the proud,
   you bring down the mighty,
   you reduce the powerful to nothing,
   choosing instead to work through those
   who seem insignificant and vulnerable.
Teach me, then,
   when I find my weaknesses hard to accept,
   to recognise that you are able to use them
   in ways beyond my imagining,
   and to understand that in those very weaknesses
   your strength is most perfectly seen.
In the name of Christ I ask it.
Amen.

363

Living God,
   I imagine sometimes that my life is in my own hands,
   mine to shape as I will.
I fondly believe myself able to meet
   the rough with the smooth,
   to withstand adversity
   and bounce back after disappointments.
On occasions it's true,
   but equally there are times when it's patently false,
   experience painfully teaching me
   how fragile is my hold on happiness
   and how limited my resources to face life's demands.
Teach me to remember that true power lies in you –
   not as the world understands it
   in any show of strength
   but in an unshakeable confidence,

an inner peace
and a living faith
through which your Spirit is able to work and move
beyond all expectations.
Open my heart to your Spirit's mighty
and mysterious presence,
and so may I discover power for living,
in Jesus' name.
Amen.

364
Living God,
I praise you for your sovereign power
through which you have transformed my life,
bringing strength, joy, hope and peace.
I thank you for the power
that flows within me through Christ
and the living presence of the Holy Spirit,
equipping me to see life in a new way
and to meet each day with confidence.
Yet I am conscious that you want
your life-changing power
to flow *through* me,
reaching out into the world beyond.
Forgive me that I have failed to let that happen,
so concerned with self
that I have forgotten my responsibility to others.
Forgive the narrowness of my vision
that has led me to store up,
rather than be a channel of,
your renewing grace.
Move within me,
and open my life to all that you are able to do,
so that in your name I may live and work for you,
through Jesus Christ my Lord.
Amen.

365
Loving God,
    for all my protestations of faith
    there are some things I consider
    to be not only beyond me but beyond you as well.
Hope says one thing but realism another,
    and in consequence I set limits
    on the way you are able to work in my life.
Forgive me for doubting your power
    and questioning your purpose.
Remind me of the way you have overturned
    human expectations throughout history,
    demonstrating that all things are possible
    for those who love you.
Teach me, then,
    to look beyond the obvious and immediate,
    and to live in the light of your sovereign grace,
    which is able to do far more
    than I can ever ask or imagine;
    through Christ my Lord.
Amen.

366
Loving God,
    there are times when you call me to tasks
    that seem beyond me,
    responsibilities I would rather avoid.
I hear your voice but I do not feel up to the challenge,
    my natural inclination being to run away.
Yet when you ask someone to do something
    you invariably give them the strength to do it.
Give me courage, then, to respond when you call,
    knowing that however things may seem,
    you are always able to transform them
    in ways far beyond my expectations.
Amen.

367

Sovereign God,
   the challenges you set before me may be very modest
   compared to those that others have faced
     over the years,
   but they can seem daunting nonetheless.
I feel inadequate to meet the task –
   acutely conscious of my lack of faith,
   the limitations of my gifts
   and my inability to serve you
   as faithfully as I would wish.
Yet, throughout history,
   you have repeatedly taken
   the most unpromising of material
   and used it in ways defying all expectations.
You have turned doubt into faith,
   weakness into strength,
   and timid service into fearless discipleship,
   and you go on doing that today
   through the power of your Holy Spirit.
Give me, then, the faith I need to respond to your call,
   trusting that, whatever you may ask of me,
   you will be by my side to help me see it through,
   to the glory of your name.
Amen.

368

Sovereign God,
   I remember how you have changed the lives
   of so many across the years,
   turning fear into courage,
   uncertainty into confidence,
   denial into affirmation.
Remind me that as you changed them,
   so you can also change me;
   that you are constantly at work

nurturing my faith,
strengthening my commitment
and deepening my experience of your love.
Open my heart to the movement of your Spirit,
    so that I may give you freedom
    to mould and shape me to your will,
    and so make me the person you would have me be,
    to your praise and glory.
Amen.

369
Living God,
    help me not to look at what I am,
    nor at what I can do,
    but rather at what you can achieve
    within me by your grace,
    through Jesus Christ my Lord.
Amen.

370
Sovereign God,
    teach me to look not at my weakness
    but at your power,
    through Jesus Christ my Lord.
Amen.

371
Sovereign God,
    teach me to let go of my fears
    and to trust in your strength,
    this day and always.
Amen.

372
Lord Jesus Christ,
    take the bruised,
    battered and broken pieces of my life,

and, by your grace,
put me together again.
Amen.

373
Lord Jesus Christ,
touch the raw spots in my life,
the aching places deep within,
and bring me the healing and wholeness
that you alone can give,
through your gracious love.
Amen.

374
Loving God,
teach me that, though my body may be broken,
my mind battered
and my spirit crushed,
you still see and value me as a whole person,
and, in that knowledge,
may I find inner healing and tranquillity,
until that day when you make me new
in your eternal kingdom,
through Jesus Christ my Lord.
Amen.

Temptation

375

Living God,

I know that much in my life is not as it should be;
that I have allowed thoughts and deeds to creep in
that inexorably eat away at my faith,
poisoning my attitudes,
and subtly destroying my relationship with you.

Help me to recognise that though you are always
ready to forgive,
such things slowly prevent me
from recognising my need for forgiveness.

Teach me that, though I cannot successfully combat
my weaknesses by myself,
with your help I can be awake to their presence
and find strength to resist them in times of temptation.

Equip me to meet whatever tests I may face
and to walk faithfully with you,
to the last.

In Christ's name I pray.

Amen.

376

Lord Jesus Christ,

you were tempted as much as anyone,
and yet you did not sin.

Forgive me that I find it so much harder
to resist temptation,
my spirit willing but my flesh weak.

Forgive me that all my resolve
can be undermined in just a few seconds
as temptation repeatedly catches me unawares.

Renew and refashion me in your image,
so that when I am tempted to go astray –

   to indulge my desires,
   ignore your will
   and excuse what I know to be inexcusable –
   I will have the inner strength to say no.
Touch my heart and put a right spirit within me,
   so that in times of trial I may stay true to your way,
   by your grace.
Amen.

377

Living God,
   there are times when I deliberately disobey you,
   but more often than not I inadvertently let you down,
   failing both you and others.
Save me from punishing myself over innocent mistakes,
   but grant me also wisdom and insight,
   so that I may be awake to temptation,
   alert to pitfalls
   and sensitive to pressures that might lead me astray.
Direct my steps,
   and help me to walk in your way,
   by your grace.
Amen.

378

Lord,
   I thank you for the privilege
   of being able to worship and witness to you freely
   and of being able to read your word
   and declare your name
   without fear of recrimination.
Save me, though, from ever imagining
   that my faith is safe from challenge.
Remind me that I am part of a world
   in which Christian values
   are constantly being undermined,

where greed and selfishness are held up as virtues,
and where wealth and success
have all too often replaced you
as the real object of humankind's devotion.
Every day the pressure is there to conform,
to give a little ground:
first here,
then there,
until little by little my convictions are diluted
and the distinctiveness of my faith destroyed.
Teach me to be awake to the dangers I face,
and give me strength to resist them
by holding fast to you.
Amen.

Thanksgiving

379
Lord,
   I have so much to thank you for,
   yet all too often I take it for granted.
Instead of counting my blessings,
   I dwell on my frustrations.
Instead of celebrating everything you have given,
   I brood about the things I don't have.
In pursuit of illusory dreams of happiness,
   I lose sight of the gifts that each day brings,
   the countless reasons I have now to rejoice.
Forgive me for forgetting how fortunate I am,
   and help me to appreciate the wonder
   of all I have received from your loving hands.
Amen.

380
Gracious God,
   you give to me out of love,
   pouring out ever more blessings day after day.
Forgive me for sometimes giving to you
   out of habit or duty.
I bring an offering in worship because it is expected.
I make time for personal devotion
   because I feel I ought to.
I respond to others only when my conscience pricks.
The results may seem worthy enough,
   but the true value is small.
Teach me instead to give joyfully,
   not because I must but because I may.
Teach me to offer my money,
   my worship and my service
   as a gesture of love and an expression of my gratitude.

Help me to understand that it is not the gift that matters
   so much as the spirit in which it is given,
   and may that awareness inspire me
   to offer myself freely to you,
   in Christ's name.
Amen.

381
Loving God,
   I have so much to thank you for –
   so much that is good and special.
Day after day you bless me,
   week after week you answer my prayers,
   year after year you meet my needs.
I cannot thank you enough for your great goodness . . .
   yet the truth is that I rarely thank you at all.
Forgive me for taking your gifts for granted,
   for letting familiarity blind me to how fortunate I am,
   and so failing to thank you for all you have given.
Forgive me for being swift to ask for your blessing
   yet slow to acknowledge your generosity in giving it.
Teach me to receive your innumerable gifts
   with heartfelt gratitude,
   and to show my thanks not just in words
   but also in my daily living –
   in a life that gratefully celebrates
   the wonder of your love.
Amen.

382
Loving God,
   teach me to celebrate all I have received,
   but to set my heart first on your kingdom
   and to show my gratitude for all your gifts
   by offering back my life in your service,
   to the glory of your name.
Amen.

383
Living God,
  help me not just to express thankfulness but also
  to show it in the most eloquent way possible:
  through joyfully receiving your gracious gifts
  and faithfully using them to serve your will
  and bring you glory.
Amen.

384
Gracious God,
  however often I thank you,
  I can never thank you enough,
  for your blessings are too many to number
  and your goodness is too wonderful for words.
So I come, as I have come so often before,
  to express my gratitude for all I have received
  from your bountiful hands.
Amen.

385
Living God,
  for the times I have forgotten to say thank you,
  and the times I have expressed gratitude
  but not really meant it, forgive me.
Receive now my grateful and heartfelt acknowledgement
  for the countless good things
  you have showered upon me.
Amen.

386
Gracious God,
  help me not only to ask in faith
  but also to receive with gratitude,
  through Jesus Christ my Lord.
Amen.

Time and eternity

387
Living God,
>   even in my lifetime so much has changed,
>   so many things that I considered permanent
>   turning out to be passing shadows.
It is hard not to be unsettled by it all,
>   and harder still not to question whether
>   anything is permanent,
>   even your love.
I find myself all at sea,
>   tossed here and there by the waves,
>   overwhelmed by a sense of helplessness
>   in stemming the relentless flow of time,
>   and I look around in desperation
>   for something to support me,
>   a lifeline to keep me afloat.
Teach me to look to you,
>   the one unchanging reality in a world
>   that is constantly moving on.
Teach me that you alone offer a hope that endures;
>   a purpose that defies the ravages of the years;
>   and so may I keep my eyes fixed on you,
>   come what may,
>   assured that though all else may fade away,
>   your love will remain the same,
>   unchanged and unchangeable.
In Christ's name I ask it.
Amen.

388
Gracious God,
>   this is the day that you have made
>   and I praise you for it.

Forgive me for so often failing to do that,
    frittering away what I have now
    through my preoccupation with what once was
    or what yet might be.
Help me to recognise each day as your gift,
    to be received with gratitude and lived to the full.
Teach me to welcome every moment as a new beginning;
    to put the past behind me,
    and work towards the future
    you hold in store.
This is the day that you have made –
    in Christ's name I will rejoice and be glad in it.
Amen.

389
Lord,
    I know it's foolish,
    that impatience gets me nowhere,
    but I just can't help it.
I try telling myself, 'What's the hurry?'
I do my best to slow down,
    to take it easy.
I remind myself of what really matters.
Yet, before I know it,
    I find myself fretting once more
    about a few moments wasted here,
    a little delay there.
Touch me by your grace
    and teach me to receive every moment as your gift,
    living each one for what it is.
Put a tranquil spirit,
    a quiet mind
    and a patient heart within me,
    and help me to learn that the more I worry about time,
    the less I will enjoy the time I have.
Amen.

390
Loving God,
  despite my faith there are times
  when I find life difficult,
  when situations seem hopeless,
  when I look to the future
  fearfully wondering what good it can possibly hold.
Help me to understand that the truth of resurrection
  is not just limited to the future,
  to life after death,
  but is about the present,
  life now!
Help me to realise it speaks not just about eternal issues
  but about daily life –
  the ordinary, the commonplace and the mundane.
Help me to understand that even there,
  and especially there,
  you bring resurrection.
Amen.

391
Lord Jesus Christ,
  you came to bring us life in all its fullness;
  to offer hope beyond the grave.
Teach me that death is not the end,
  but a new beginning –
  the gateway to life everlasting.
And may that confidence shape my attitude
  not only towards death
  but towards life also.
May I live each day not just in the context
  of the here and now but of eternity,
  knowing there is nothing in heaven or earth
  that shall ever finally be able
  to separate me from your love.
Amen.

392
Loving God,
    I thank you for all the ways you are with me
    and all the ways you grant your blessing.
I thank you for the guidance you give,
    the strength you supply,
    the mercy you show
    and the love with which you surround me.
I thank you that your purpose extends
    beyond this life into eternity;
    that you are holding the best in store.
Teach me to walk with you each day
    knowing you are always by my side,
    and so may I trust you for the future,
    secure in the everlasting hope
    you have given in Christ.
Amen.

393
God of past, present and future,
    help me to remember all you have done,
    to rejoice in all you are doing,
    and to trust in all you will yet do.
Teach me to put my hand in yours
    and to walk with you wherever you may lead,
    knowing that you will walk by my side,
    this day and always.
Amen.

394
Eternal God,
    teach me to use each moment wisely,
    open to your guidance,
    alert to your will.
Teach me to see time not as a threat but as your gift,
    and so may I live life to the full, as you desire.
Amen.

395
Sovereign God,
    when I start to fret over the loss of a single minute,
    remind me that your love will continue for all eternity.
Amen.

396
Lord Jesus Christ,
    may new life be born within me this and every day,
    and may your life-giving hope sustain me
    through the joys and sorrows of this world,
    until that time when I pass through the shadow of
    death into the light of your eternal kingdom.
Amen.

397
Lord Jesus Christ,
    teach me that whatever today may hold
    and whatever tomorrow might bring,
    the future is secure, for you are with me,
    the same yesterday, today and for ever.
Help me, then, to live each moment with you,
    in quiet confidence and joyful celebration,
    knowing I am yours and you are mine,
    for all eternity.
Amen.

398
Living God,
    where death casts its shadow over life,
    seeming to block out all rays of hope,
    remind me of your promised kingdom
    in which there will be no more night,
    nor need for lamp or sun,
    for your light will be all in all,
    shining for evermore.
Amen.

True satisfaction

399
Living God,
  I like to imagine that possessions don't matter to me
  but the reality is different.
I surround myself with all kinds of belongings
  and I am constantly seeking more.
Some contribute much to my life,
  others yield nothing,
  but all of them can so easily keep me from you,
  closing my eyes to what is
  ultimately important in life.
Forgive me the time,
  money and resources I waste
  in accumulating what I do not need.
Forgive the selfishness
  and the wasted opportunities to give to
  or serve others that all this entails.
Teach me to travel light,
  recognising where true fulfilment lies,
  and so may my service be deepened
  and my relationship with you enriched.
Amen.

400
Living God,
  you have taught me that I should
  long to know you better:
  not just to want that
  but to urgently,
  passionately
  and wholeheartedly yearn for it,
  striving with all my being to understand your will
  and fulfil your purpose.

You have told me that those who hunger and thirst
    after righteousness will be filled.
Teach me the secret of such hunger.
Instead of cluttering my life
    with so much that can never satisfy,
    teach me to empty myself
    so that I may be filled by you;
    to desire your kingdom,
    seek your will
    and study your word,
    earnestly,
    eagerly,
    expectantly.
However much I know of your love,
    however richly you may have blessed me,
    teach me to keep that hunger alive,
    to thirst always for a deepening of my faith,
    a strengthening of my service
    and a greater awareness of your purpose,
    through Jesus Christ my Lord.
Amen.

401
Lord Jesus Christ,
    I have no need to be thirsty,
    for I have tasted the living water you offer
    and experienced first-hand its power to satisfy,
    yet sometimes I turn my back
    on the life-giving spring you offer.
I seek fulfilment elsewhere –
    in money,
    possessions,
    work,
    friendships –
    forgetting that none of these,

however much pleasure they may bring,
    can meet my deepest needs.
Help me to enjoy the blessings you have given,
    the innumerable good things in life,
    but help me also to keep a proper sense of perspective,
    recognising that you are the one
    who gives meaning to all.
So may the water of life well up within me
    and overflow in joyful praise,
    loving service
    and spontaneous witness,
    to the glory of your name.
Amen.

402
Eternal God,
    I spend so much of my life seeking happiness,
    yet much of the time I am frustrated.
I turn from one thing to another,
    believing for a moment
    that it may offer the fulfilment I crave,
    but so many pleasures are fleeting,
    here today and gone tomorrow.
There are times when life seems empty,
    when nothing seems permanent,
    not even those things most precious to me.
Help me to find the rest for my soul
    that you alone can give;
    to discover in you that inner peace
    which can never change
    but which will go on satisfying for all eternity.
Help me to live each day in tune with you,
    rejoicing in all you have given
    and anticipating all you have yet to give,
    through Christ my Lord.
Amen.

403
Loving God,
　　thank you for your great gift of life in all its fullness –
　　everything you have given to enjoy,
　　celebrate
　　and live for.
Thank you for the innumerable blessings
　　you shower upon me every day:
　　love to share,
　　beauty to enthral,
　　health to enjoy,
　　food to eat
　　and so much more –
　　a world to excite, fascinate and savour.
Above all, thank you for the life
　　you have given me in Christ;
　　a life that you want me and all people to enjoy
　　not just now but for all eternity.
Teach me to celebrate your love in all its richness,
　　to rejoice in your gifts in all their abundance
　　and to celebrate life in all its fullness,
　　to the glory of your name.
Amen.

404
Living God,
　　I thank you that you provide me
　　not only with daily bread
　　but also with the bread of life –
　　inner nourishment that means
　　I need never go spiritually hungry again.
You offer so much to nourish my faith:
　　your love in Christ,
　　the inner presence of your Holy Spirit,
　　and the testimony of the scriptures –
　　and yet all too often I fail to feed myself as I should.

The result is that I grow weak instead of strong,
   my faith starved,
   emaciated,
   wasting away –
   a pale shadow of what it ought to be.
Forgive me,
   and teach me to nurture my faith
   so that I may be strong in your service,
   to your glory.
Amen.

Witnessing

405
Lord Jesus Christ,
    just as others have introduced you to me,
    so help me in turn to introduce you to others:
    not preaching at them,
    nor seeking to ram my beliefs down their throats,
    nor trying to argue with them
    or to convince them of the claims of the gospel,
    but simply pointing at who and what you are.
Help me to speak of all that you mean to me
    and of everything I have found you to be,
    and so may others come to meet you
    and know you for themselves,
    through your grace.
Amen.

406
Lord Jesus Christ,
    you call me,
    as you call all your people,
    to go out and proclaim the gospel.
You expect me not simply to believe the good news,
    but also to share it.
Forgive me for failing to honour that calling;
    for being only too ready to come to you
    but less willing to go out in your name;
    eager to receive but reluctant to give.
Help me to recognise my responsibility towards others –
    to understand that if I leave it to someone else
    to tell them about Jesus,
    they may never hear the good news.
Help me to understand that discipleship without service
    is no discipleship at all,

and that faith without witness
is a denial of everything I claim to believe.
Fill me, then, with new vision and resolve,
so that when the opportunity comes to speak for you,
I may do so –
faithfully,
honestly,
sensitively
and joyfully –
to the glory of your name.
Amen.

407

Lord Jesus Christ,
you have called me to be your witness,
to proclaim your name and make known your love,
but, though I try to respond to that challenge,
I find it so hard.
When I speak of you I am met with indifference,
even hostility.
Though I keep on trying,
in my heart I give up,
no longer expecting lives to be changed by your word.
Teach me to look beyond appearances
and to recognise that,
though I may not always see it,
the seed I sow
often bears fruit in unexpected ways and places;
that though much will fall on barren soil,
some will find fertile ground
and in the fullness of time bear a rich harvest.
Help me to trust not in my ability
but in your life-giving power, confident that,
if *I* play my part, *you* will play yours.
In your name I ask it.
Amen.

408
Sovereign God,
 you have given me so much to share,
 more than I can ever begin to express.
You have showered me with your blessings,
 touching my life in innumerable ways.
You have given me a joy that knows no bounds,
 mercy beyond all my deserving,
 hope that can never be exhausted,
 peace that passes understanding
 and love that exceeds anything
 I can ever ask or think of.
Teach me to share that with others,
 to tell joyfully and spontaneously
 of everything you have done
 and of all you mean to me,
 to the glory of your name.
Amen.

409
Living God,
 it isn't easy to speak out against wrong.
I prefer to mind my own business
 rather than get involved;
 to keep my head down for fear of the possible
 consequences should I intervene.
More than that, I hold back for fear of hypocrisy,
 being all too conscious of my own faults and failings,
 and thus feeling I have no right to judge others.
For good or bad reasons,
 from the best or worst of motives,
 I am sometimes silent,
 allowing evil to go unchallenged,
 rather than lifting up my voice against it.
Help me to know when it is not only right
 but necessary to speak,

and when such moments come,
give me wisdom, sensitivity and courage,
so that I will know the words to say
and be enabled to say them.
Give me that rare ability to speak the truth in love,
through Jesus Christ my Lord.
Amen.

410
Sovereign God,
when you give me your word,
give me the courage I need to speak it.
Amen.

411
Lord Jesus Christ,
whenever I speak for you,
save me from trying to be clever;
help me simply to be genuine.
Amen.

412
Gracious God,
help me to be fully involved in this world
and yet to live also in the light of the world to come,
and so may my life witness to your sovereign
purpose and your saving love.
Amen.

413
Living God,
may my lips speak of you,
my deeds honour you,
and my life proclaim you.
Amen.

414

Lord Jesus Christ,
  you have touched my heart,
  brought me joy and given me life in all its fullness.
Equip me now, through your Spirit,
  to make you known and to share with others
  the blessing I have found in you,
  for your name's sake.
  Amen.

415

Sovereign God,
  whenever and wherever there is opportunity,
  teach me to witness in a way
  that is relevant and alive,
  speaking eagerly,
  faithfully and honestly of everything
  that you have done for me in Christ,
  and so may your gracious love
  be made known to all.
Amen.

416

Lord Jesus Christ,
  teach me when to speak of you
  and when to remain silent,
  when to share my faith
  and when to leave things in your hands.
Help me to know when each time may be
  and to respond accordingly,
  for your name's sake.
Amen.

417

Lord Jesus Christ,
  show me when and where to speak for you,

but remind me, having spoken,
that you are also able to speak for yourself.
Amen.

418
Lord Jesus Christ,
teach me to sow the seed of your word,
confident that you will nurture it
until the time is ripe for harvest.
Amen.